74.7
ste

6504

6504

DATE DUE

Metro Litho
Oak Forest, IL 60452

SEP 18 1992			

AMERICA the BEAUTIFUL

NEW YORK

By R. Conrad Stein

Consultants

Donald H. Bragaw, Ph.D., Chief, Bureau of Social Studies Education, New York State Education Department

Paul J. Scudiere, Ed.D., State Historian, New York State Museum, Albany

Robert L. Hillerich, Ph.D., Bowling Green State University, Bowling Green, Ohio

CHILDRENS PRESS®

CHICAGO

A mansion in the Finger Lakes region

Project Editor: Joan Downing
Assistant Editor: Shari Joffe
Design Director: Margrit Fiddle
Typesetting: Graphic Connections, Inc.
Engraving: Liberty Photoengraving

THIRD PRINTING, 1992.
INCLUDES 1990 CENSUS FIGURES.

Childrens Press®, Chicago
Copyright ©1989 by Regensteiner Publishing Enterprises, Inc.
All rights reserved. Published simultaneously in Canada.
Printed in the United States of America.
  3 4 5 6 7 8 9 10 R 98 97 96 95 94 93 92 91

Library of Congress Cataloging-in-Publication Data

Stein, R. Conrad.
  America the beautiful. New York / by R. Conrad Stein.
    p.   cm.
  Includes index.
  Summary: Introduces the geography, history,
government, economy, industry, culture, historic sites,
and famous people of this large state of diverse
populations.
  ISBN 0-516-00478-6
  1. New York (State)—Juvenile literature. [1. New
York (State)] I. Title.
F119.3.S74   1988   88-11748
974.7—dc19   CIP
                                                   AC

A mountain climber
tackles the
Shawangunk Mountains.

TABLE OF CONTENTS

Chapter 1

AMERICA'S FRONT DOOR

AMERICA'S FRONT DOOR

A visitor to New York's Manhattan Island once wrote that he heard eighteen different languages spoken on the streets. This comment was not made in modern times, although today nearly every language known to the world is spoken in Manhattan. Instead the visitor was a Dutch official, and he made his observation in the year 1644.

Since its beginning as a Dutch colony, New York has acted as a gateway to the New World. Over the years, millions of immigrants have come to America through New York City, the state's vast Atlantic Ocean port. While many newcomers have simply passed through the state, others have stayed to give New York one of the most diverse populations in the world.

The state's landforms and institutions reflect the variety of its people. New York has wild mountain ranges, rolling hills, and miles of lonely beaches. It is a giant in industry, agriculture, business, and culture. New York State has many quiet small towns as well as the nation's largest and most exciting city. Its natural beauty and its energetic people give credence to its nickname—the Empire State.

Chapter 2
THE LAND

THE LAND

GEOGRAPHY

New York is a mid-Atlantic state, but only its southern tip actually touches the ocean. Nestled on that tip, however, is New York City, which has one of the world's largest natural harbors. The harbor areas of London, Hamburg, Amsterdam, and Antwerp could all fit into New York harbor with room to spare.

Roughly, New York State is shaped like an old-fashioned, high-top shoe. On a map, the heel of the shoe seems to be stamping into the Atlantic Ocean, while fish-shaped Long Island swims for cover.

In the north, a human-made boundary line separates New York from the Canadian province of Quebec. To the west, the St. Lawrence River, Lake Ontario, the Niagara River, and Lake Erie complete the state's border with Canada. To the south, Pennsylvania and New Jersey are its neighbors. Along New York's eastern border lie Connecticut, Massachusetts, and Vermont.

Albany is the state's capital; New York is its largest city.

New York has a total area of 49,108 square miles (127,189 square kilometers), ranking thirtieth among the states in size. Its greatest distances are 409 miles (658 kilometers) east to west, and 307 miles (494 kilometers) north to south.

The words *upstate* and *downstate* are frequently used to describe locations in New York State, but there is no agreement about what the words mean. Some people offer a precise definition: Draw an arc from Binghamton to Albany, and everything south and east of the arc is downstate, while the land north and west of the arc is considered upstate. Others believe the terms refer to a state of mind rather than an exact location: Anything that is rural and beyond the New York City suburbs is called upstate, while communities near the big city are referred to as downstate.

New York City is an exciting place to visit, but its geography can be confusing to outsiders. The city is composed of five distinct boroughs, each with its own personality. The boroughs are Manhattan, the Bronx, Brooklyn, Queens, and Staten Island. Only the Bronx is part of the mainland. Brooklyn and Queens are part of Long Island and Staten Island and Manhattan are separate islands.

LANDFORMS AND LAND USE

New York is composed of seven major land areas: the St. Lawrence Lowland in the north, a flat strip that hugs the St. Lawrence River; the Adirondack Upland in the northeast, which includes the 5,344-foot (1,629-meter) Mount Marcy, the tallest mountain in the state; the Great Lakes Lowland, sometimes called the Erie-Ontario Lowland, which is a flat area that rings the shores of Lake Ontario and Lake Erie; the Hudson-Mohawk Lowland, which covers the valleys carved out by the Hudson and

Dairy farming thrives in the Appalachian Plateau, and the land along the Great Lakes Lowland produces bountiful grape harvests.

Mohawk rivers; the New England Upland, which includes the Taconic Mountains along the state's eastern border; the Atlantic Coastal Plain, the lowland area that makes up Long Island and Staten Island; and the Appalachian Plateau, the state's largest land area, which takes in most of southern New York.

More than half of New York State is covered by forests where deer, bear, fox, mink, and countless other wild creatures can be found. Many woodlands are in private hands and are harvested by lumber companies. New York also boasts 150 state parks and 60 forest areas, all of which are open to the public.

The Empire State has about ten million acres (four million hectares) of farmland. Some of its richest soil is found along the Hudson and Mohawk rivers. The soil in the Appalachian Plateau in south-central New York is less fertile, but dairy farming and cattle raising thrive there. The land along the Great Lakes Lowland produces fruit such as apples, pears, and grapes.

COASTLANDS AND ISLANDS

New York is the only American state that touches both the Atlantic Ocean and the Great Lakes. This geographical fact allowed the Empire State to become a vital link between the Atlantic seaboard and midwestern America. New York City is the state's principal port on the Atlantic; Oswego and Rochester are Lake Ontario ports; Buffalo serves Lake Erie.

True to its name, Long Island is about 130 miles (209 kilometers) long and only 23 miles (37 kilometers) across at its widest point. New York City's Manhattan Island is 13 miles (21 kilometers) long and 2.5 miles (4 kilometers) wide. There are many islands in the Great Lakes region, including Thousand Islands, a popular vacation area located where Lake Ontario meets the St. Lawrence River.

RIVERS AND LAKES

The Hudson River originates high in the Adirondack Mountains and flows due south to empty into the Atlantic Ocean at New York City. The Mohawk, the Hudson's principal tributary, begins at Albany and winds through central New York. The two river valleys have been important avenues in the state's history, serving as trade routes for Indian merchants and as pathways for canal, railroad, and highway builders. The Oswego, the Genesee, the Seneca, the Delaware, and the Allegheny are other major rivers.

Niagara Falls is one of New York's most popular vacation spots, but the state has many other waterfalls, including the stately Taughannock Falls near Cayuga Lake, northwest of Ithaca, and the eighteen waterfalls on the grounds of Watkins Glen State Park.

Times Square, New York City, after a winter snowstorm

Thousands of years ago, New York was covered by glaciers that gouged pits into the land—pits that later became about eight thousand lakes. Lake Champlain's coastline is shared with Vermont. Lake Oneida near Syracuse is the largest lake within the state. To the west lie six narrow sheets of deep, blue water called the Finger Lakes.

CLIMATE

Much of upstate New York suffers harsh winters. The Adirondack Mountains were once called "America's Siberia." Great Lakes cities such as Buffalo and Rochester are often buried under pelting snowstorms. Syracuse averages 108 inches (274 centimeters) of snow a year, more than any other American city. To the south, however, warm ocean currents ease winter's chill in New York City and other Atlantic Coastal Plain communities. The average January temperature is 32 degrees Fahrenheit (0 degrees Celsius) in New York City, while mountain communities farther north are almost twice as cold.

Among New York's many free-flowing rivers is the Ausable, in the Adirondacks.

During the summer, New York City dwellers endure day after day of sultry heat, but in the Catskill Mountains, just a few hours' drive north, the temperatures are delightfully cool. The highest temperature ever recorded in New York occurred in the Hudson River city of Troy, where the temperature soared to 108 degrees Fahrenheit (42 degrees Celsius) in July 1926. The lowest temperature reading was taken just a few miles north of Troy, when the mercury plunged to minus 52 degrees Fahrenheit (minus 47 degrees Celsius) in January 1979.

New York's many lakes and free-flowing rivers attest to the fact that plenty of water falls in the state. Overall, the state averages 32 to 54 inches (81 to 137 centimeters) of total precipitation (a combination of rain and snow) each year. By contrast, many areas of Oklahoma average only 15 inches (38 centimeters) of total precipitation. Despite generous rainfall, a stubborn drought plagued New York City during the early 1980s. Some New Yorkers actually performed rain dances while trying to coax a few drops from the cloudless sky.

Chapter 3
THE PEOPLE

THE PEOPLE

. . . Give me your tired, your poor,
Your huddled masses yearning to breathe free . . .
—From the Emma Lazarus poem inscribed on the Statue
of Liberty, which towers over New York Harbor

WHO ARE THE NEW YORKERS?

People of nearly every race and national heritage live in New York. There are more blacks than in any other state, more Jews than in any other state, and more Puerto Ricans than in any other state. More than sixty thousand Native Americans live in New York.

New York City is an ethnic potpourri. The city and its suburbs hold more Italians than Naples, more Irish than Dublin, and more Greeks than any city outside of Athens. More than half a million Asians and many thousands of Cubans, Haitians, and Dominicans also live in New York City.

America is a multicultural country—a place where men and women of different skin colors and varying ethnic backgrounds manage to live together. Probably no other state has a greater ethnic and racial mix than does New York.

POPULATION AND POPULATION DISTRIBUTION

From 1820 until 1963, New York was the most populous state in the nation. But California has enjoyed explosive growth, and its population has surpassed that of New York. In 1990, New York's

population stood at 17,990,455, placing it a distant second to California. The number of people in the Empire State increased only 2.5 percent from 1980 to 1990. But despite this, New York boasts the nation's number one city.

Gigantic and bustling New York City is often called the "Big Apple." And it certainly is big. Including its suburbs, New York City's population tops eight million. It is by far the largest city in the United States, and it ranks ninth in the world. Only eight states, not including New York, have populations that exceed that of New York City.

Population in upstate New York is concentrated along the Mohawk and Hudson river valleys. In or near those valleys lie the cities of Albany, Schenectady, Amsterdam, Utica, Rome, Syracuse, Rochester, and Buffalo. With more than a million people in its metropolitan area, Buffalo is the state's second-largest city.

A pleasant mixture of towns, farms, and woodland spreads along the state's long southern border with Pennsylvania, which New Yorkers call the southern tier. Binghamton and Elmira are the southern tier's leading cities. The state's least-populated regions are the far northern tip and the rugged Adirondack Mountains.

New Yorkers' diverse religious preferences reflect the
diversity of the state's population. Shown here are New
York City's landmark St. Patrick's Cathedral (above), the
seat of the Roman Catholic Archdiocese of New York;
Brooklyn's Williamsburg neighborhood, which is the home
of a large population of Hasidic Jews (right); and a
Russian Orthodox church in upstate Herkimer (top right).

RELIGION

New York has more Roman Catholics than any other state—
about 6.5 million (37 percent of the state's population). Other
leading Christian churches include Episcopalian, Methodist,
Lutheran, Presbyterian, and Greek Orthodox.

Fully 15 percent of the state's people are Jews, and most of them
live in the New York City area. The Islamic and Buddhist faiths
have large followings in New York, and there are also many
smaller religious sects.

The multilingual makeup of New York City is apparent in the signs seen in various neighborhoods. On Manhattan's Lower East Side, for instance, Hebrew signs are common (far left), and in Brooklyn's Brighton Beach neighborhood (left), Russian and Spanish signs are prevalent.

LANGUAGES

Each newly arriving group of immigrants brought to New York its own language, or its own way of speaking English. A walk down the streets of New York City confirms that a world of languages remains the rule today. Spanish is the city's most prominent language other than English; but around one corner Greek is spoken, around another corner, Italian, and around still another corner, Vietnamese. A generation ago, the state was even more multilingual than it is today. Polish used to be heard more frequently than English in Buffalo neighborhoods, and Irish brogues once rang out in every borough.

New York City dwellers have long been famous for their expressions and sometimes for their pronunciation. New Yorkers *stand on* line; nearly everyone else *waits in* line. A million jokes have been told about "Toity-toid Street and Toid Avenue." Yiddish words such as *schmaltzy* (overly sentimental) have worked their way from New York City sidewalks into the American language.

Chapter 4
THE BEGINNING

THE BEGINNING

*The land of Ganono-o or 'Empire State,' as you
love to call it, was once laced by our trails from
Albany to Buffalo—trails that we had trod for
centuries—trails worn so deep by the feet of the
Iroquois that they became your own roads of travel. . . .*
—A Cayuga chief addressing the New York
Historical Society in 1847

THE ORIGINAL NEW YORKERS

For untold centuries, most of New York was covered by a
blanket of ice that measured up to two miles (three kilometers)
thick. When the ice retreated northward about ten thousand years
ago, forests sprouted up. Into the forests moved people who, some
scientists believe, had migrated to the New World from Asia.
Those men and women were the true discoverers of America.
Christopher Columbus later mistakenly called their descendants
Indians.

The first New Yorkers were hunters who followed the herds of
enormous mammoths and mastodons that once inhabited the
state. Archaeologists still find spearpoints and stone knives left by
those early people.

About A.D. 700, a remarkable civilization called the Mound
Builders flourished in the Mississippi and Ohio valleys. These
people built complex earthen mounds shaped like pyramids or
animals and used these structures as burial sites and places of

worship. The Mound Builders' influence extended as far east as
New York, and some of their earthwork figures have been
uncovered within the state.

In the years before contact with Europeans, New York was
inhabited mainly by five tribes of Algonquian-speaking people
and the five tribes that made up the Iroquois Nation. The
Algonquian group included the Delaware, Mohican, Wappinger,
Montauk, and Munsee. They lived along the banks of the lower
Hudson River and occupied Staten Island, Long Island, and
Manhattan. The Iroquois lived in upstate New York.

THE WORLD OF THE IROQUOIS

The roots of the Iroquois Nation were formed long before the
coming of Europeans. Five tribes—the Mohawk, the Oneida, the
Onondaga, the Cayuga, and the Seneca—once lived in the forests
of upstate New York, where they waged wars so savage that the
groups almost faced extinction. Then a mysterious outsider called
the Peacemaker appeared. According to legend, he rode in a canoe
made of a curious white stone. The Peacemaker befriended an
Onondaga named Hiawatha—whom poet Henry Wadsworth
Longfellow later mistakenly placed in Minnesota—and together
they convinced the five tribes to stop making war and form the
Iroquois Confederacy, or League of the Five Nations. The rules of
the confederation gave each tribe a degree of independence, but a
Great Council made up of all the tribes had supreme authority.
Historians believe the federation was established about 1570, but
Iroquois legends put the date at least a thousand years earlier.

Is the United States Constitution a gift from the Iroquois?
Certainly the federation formed by the thirteen American colonies
was similar to that established by the Iroquois groups. It is known

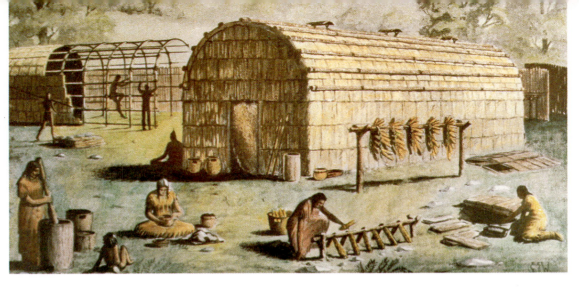

The Iroquois constructed sturdy and distinctive homes called long houses.

that James Madison, the "Architect of the Constitution," studied Iroquois government. Some historians believe the American form of government was modeled after the ancient Iroquois Nation.

The Iroquois lived in long wooden houses and called themselves the *Haudenosaunee*, or "long-house builders." They hunted and fished, but were also splendid farmers. French explorers marveled at their orderly fields, which stretched for miles. They relied so heavily on corn, beans, and squash that these three crops were known as the "three sisters of the Iroquois."

A sternly religious people, the Iroquois worshiped a single creator and a host of lesser gods and spirits. To them, all living things—including animals and trees—had souls that went on to another life after death. Iroquois women had a major say in tribal decision making and assisted in all religious ceremonies. Women arranged marriages and approved or denied divorces. Children inherited their mother's, not their father's, family name.

Although they refused to wage war against each other, the tribes of the Iroquois Nation fought their neighbors with fury. None of their rivals was able to match the bravery and military organization of the Iroquois. At the height of its power, the Iroquois Nation spread from the Atlantic Ocean to the Mississippi River and from Tennessee north to Canada.

THE EXPLORERS

In 1524, Italian sea captain Giovanni Da Verrazano became the first European to enter New York's harbor. Gazing at the mouth of the Hudson, he wrote, "We found a very pleasant place, situated amongst certain little steep hills, and there ran down into the sea a great river." Verrazano also found a welcoming committee made up of Algonquian canoes. "They came toward us very cheerfully, making great sounds of admiration, showing us where we might come to land most safely with our boat."

In 1609, Henry Hudson, an Englishman employed by the Dutch, sailed up the broad river that now bears his name. At the site of present-day Albany, he found the junction at which the Mohawk River forms a Y with the Hudson. Impressed with the fertile river valleys, Hudson returned to Holland with a glowing report.

Also in 1609, French explorer Samuel de Champlain hiked south into New York from his base camp in Canada. In the forests near what is now Lake Champlain, he and his party fired muskets at a band of Iroquois warriors. Two Indians fell dead, and the others ran terrified into the woods. Never before had they witnessed the power of the "thunder sticks" carried by white men. This skirmish turned out to be a pivotal battle in North American history. The Iroquois never forgot and never forgave, and from that day forward were mortal enemies of the French.

The European explorers of North America sought a passage through the continent that would allow them to sail to the rich trading ports in Asia. Although they found no such seaway, they discovered that New World forests teemed with beaver and other furbearing animals. In Europe, fur hats were literally worth their weight in gold. Over the next 150 years, the Dutch, the French, and the British gained vast fortunes in the fur trade.

According to legend, the Dutch purchased Manhattan from an Algonquian Indian group for trinkets worth about $24.

THE DUTCH PERIOD

In 1624, the Dutch West India Company settled eighteen families at Fort Orange, a crude structure built where the city of Albany now stands. A year later, another shipload of Dutch colonists landed at the southern tip of the wooded island the Indians called *Man-a-hat-ta* (land of hills). It is said that the Dutch bought the entire island from an Algonquian group for trinkets valued at $24. If true, the purchase was the greatest real-estate bargain in history. The Dutch called the New York region New Netherland, and named their island settlement New Amsterdam.

To obtain beaver pelts, the Dutch exchanged goods, including guns, with the Iroquois. Armed with those guns, Iroquois warriors spread terror over half a continent. Meanwhile, the Algonquians were subdued by their old enemies, the Iroquois, and their new neighbors, the Dutch.

By 1660, the Dutch had turned New Amsterdam into a small town of three hundred houses, several churches, and a windmill. On the town's northern border stood a wall designed to keep out marauding Indians. The wall was later replaced by a road known to this day as Wall Street. Farther north on the island was the

When Dutch governor Peter Stuyvesant (with cane) was forced to surrender New Amsterdam to the English in 1664, the name of the colony was changed to New York, in honor of James, Duke of York.

farming community of Haarlem. Across the East River stood the town of Breuklyn, and beyond the Harlem River a village grew around a farm owned by Jonas Bronk. This community later became the borough known as the Bronx. Dutch farms also spread along the Hudson River from New Amsterdam to Fort Orange.

While the character of New Netherland was unmistakably Dutch, the region was thronged with British, Irish, Germans, Danes, French, Swedes, blacks, and various Indian groups. Every incoming ship brought new people to add to the ethnic mix.

Most numerous of the non-Dutch were English people who had established colonies both north and south of New Netherland. In the mid-1660s, English families from the New England colonies of Connecticut and Massachusetts settled in various parts of New Netherland. Transplanted New Englanders, called Yankees, later pioneered a bold civilization in the New York wilderness.

In Europe, war broke out between England and The Netherlands. The British king, Charles II, decided to seize New Netherland, and in 1664 his fleet sailed into New Amsterdam's harbor. Peter Stuyvesant, the Dutch governor, was hopelessly outgunned and surrendered the colony without firing a shot. The British takeover of New Netherland was engineered by the king's brother, James, the Duke of York and Albany. In his honor, Fort Orange was renamed Albany, and the name New Amsterdam was changed to New York. The Dutch briefly reoccupied their old colony in 1673, but soon the region again rested firmly in British hands.

AN ENGLISH COLONY

The British were gracious in victory. The conquerors allowed Dutch settlers to keep their land and preserve their institutions. The Dutch language was widely spoken in New York until the nineteenth century. Wealthy Dutch families such as the Van Cortlandts, the Van Rensselaers, the Schuylers, and the Stuyvesants continued to wield power and influence over the government. Two centuries later, offspring of another prominent Dutch family, the Van Roosevelts, influenced the American scene.

A famous trial was held in 1734 after newspaper owner John Peter Zenger was jailed for criticizing the New York government. Zenger continued writing his newspaper from his jail cell and was later declared not guilty. The case was a landmark in American history, for it established the tradition of a free press.

By the mid-1700s, thirteen English colonies stretched along the Atlantic seaboard from what is now Maine to Georgia. In terms of population, New York ranked seventh of the thirteen. New York City and Albany were its only cities, and Albany was little more than a village. Fur-trading posts were established at Oswego and Fort Stanwix (now the city of Rome), a whaling port grew at Long Island's Sag Harbor, and a score of farming villages dotted the shores of the Hudson.

Historians give two primary reasons for the slow growth of colonial New York. First, New York's western frontier was a battleground where the French and their Algonquian allies fought the British and their Iroquois friends. Second, colonial New York clung to the Dutch patroon system, which discouraged small farmers from coming to the colony because the best land was already held by a few wealthy families.

New York City ranked behind Philadelphia as the second-largest city in the colonies. At the time, the city was confined to the southern tip of Manhattan Island. New York was known as a rough-and-tumble seaport town with a tavern in nearly every building. Traders from other colonies feared visiting New York City because they believed criminals lurked on every street corner.

Over a period of seventy-five years, Britain and France fought four wars to determine the control of the fur trade in the New World. The last of these conflicts (called the French and Indian War in America and the Seven Years' War in Europe) ended with a British victory in 1763. Great Britain won the long struggle largely because of the fighting fury of its Iroquois allies. The Iroquois Nation's hatred of the French had never ebbed.

The French and Indian Wars emptied the treasury of Great Britain. In order to raise money, the British king decided to tax his American colonies. It was a fateful decision. Taxes on items such as tea and legal documents infuriated the colonists and ultimately led to war and the birth of a new nation.

THE REVOLUTIONARY WAR

The American Revolution is often looked upon as a great patriotic effort that pitted all Americans against their British overlords. In truth, however, many Americans were Loyalists: citizens who remained loyal to the British crown even during the height of the fighting. New York probably had more Loyalists

After the historic 1777 Battle of Saratoga, defeated British general John Burgoyne offered his sword in surrender to American general Horatio Gates.

than any other colony. As a result, New Yorkers were forced to fight two wars—one against the British and a second against one another.

New York was situated between the southern colonies and New England. British army leaders planned to occupy New York and thereby divide the American rebels. Because of this strategy, nearly one third of the war's battles were fought in New York.

Fighting began in 1776 in New York with General George Washington's defeat on Long Island. The British then captured New York City, which they occupied for the next seven years. An important part of the British plan was the capture of Albany, but American forces blocked British ships by stretching an enormous chain across the Hudson River. In 1777, two major battles were fought at the tiny New York towns of Saratoga and Oriskany. The Battle of Saratoga was a turning point in the war, and one of history's most decisive battles. Not only did the British lose at Saratoga, but when France heard of the defeat, she joined the war on the American side.

The murder of Jane McCrea by Iroquois scouts under the command of British officers so outraged New Yorkers that General George Washington sent an army to destroy the Iroquois.

Meanwhile, a sporadic but bloody war raged on New York's western frontier as British-led Iroquois warriors ravaged farm settlements. Many Loyalists fought alongside the British and the Iroquois. New Yorkers were outraged when Iroquois scouts under the command of British officers murdered a woman named Jane McCrea. The senseless crime rallied New Yorkers against the Iroquois and the Loyalists. General Washington sent an army to the Finger Lakes region to smash the Iroquois. The army did its job so thoroughly that the mighty Iroquois Nation never rose again. After the war, thirty thousand New York Loyalists fled the state.

When peace was declared, the new American government was based briefly in New York. The United States Constitution was ratified by New York in the town of Poughkeepsie on July 26, 1788. Two New Yorkers—John Jay and Alexander Hamilton— contributed to an important series of essays called *The Federalist*, which urged other Americans to accept the authority of the federal government. New York City served as the nation's capital from January 1785 to March 1789, and George Washington was inaugurated there as the country's first president.

Chapter 5
THE SEAT OF AN EMPIRE

THE SEAT OF AN EMPIRE

During the height of the revolutionary war, General George Washington toured New York and boldly claimed that it would one day become the seat of a new empire. Thus New York received its nickname, the Empire State. At the time, New York was a backward region, but a brilliant future lay just ahead.

SETTLING THE WEST

Beyond the Appalachian Mountains spread the untamed Iroquois lands. A state agency called the New York Land Board bought most of the land from the defeated Iroquois, carved it up into townships, and offered it to settlers at low prices. The Land Board gave classical Greek and Roman names to some of the townships—Rome, Ithaca, and Syracuse. War veterans were awarded generous farms in the west in return for their years of service. Many wealthy speculators snapped up the land and held onto it, waiting for prices to rise. Even George Washington bought land in New York.

A fresh wave of Yankee farmers purchased much of the inexpensive land in the west. Many New Yorkers looked on the transplanted New Englanders as unwanted intruders. Writer James Fenimore Cooper called them "those locusts of the west." But the Yankees were experienced in establishing pioneer villages, and were quick to build schools in their communities. Troy,

Hudson, Buffalo, Syracuse, Rochester, Utica, and a dozen other upstate towns owe their early growth to Yankee farmers.

The War of 1812, fought between the United States and Great Britain, put a temporary halt to western expansion. Once again, New York became a battlefield as British forces from Canada attacked and burned Fort Niagara and the towns of Buffalo, Black Rock, and Lewiston. To the northeast, a major battle was fought at Plattsburgh, on the shores of Lake Champlain.

The land rush on New York's western frontier gained new strength after the War of 1812. Soon the forests were being cleared and land was being farmed by half a million settlers. The 1820 census showed that New York's population had surged to 1,372,812, moving the Empire State to first place in the country. And a bold project soon propelled the state and the nation into a prosperous new era.

THE ERIE CANAL

For years, Americans had dreamed of building an overland canal that would connect the Atlantic Ocean with the Great Lakes. New York's Mohawk Valley was a logical path for such a waterway, but enormous obstacles barred its construction. Such a canal would have to stretch hundreds of miles through forests and swamps and somehow cross the Appalachian Mountains. President Thomas Jefferson, whose ideas were usually a generation ahead of his time, said of the proposed canal, "It is a splendid project and may be executed a century hence. . . . But it is a little short of madness to think of it at this day!"

Nevertheless, New York's governor, De Witt Clinton, believed the canal could be built, and he possessed the stubborn courage to fight for its construction. Clinton, whose uncle was the state's first governor, had been born into a wealthy New York family. He was tall, ruggedly handsome, and a splendid speaker. Many believed he could become president of the United States. Instead, he devoted his energies to building what his critics called "Clinton's Ditch." History would call it the Erie Canal.

The federal government refused to spend a dime on the canal project, so Clinton appealed to the New York State Legislature for funds. He argued that tolls collected on the canal would more than pay for the cost of construction. He further claimed that the canal would stimulate the state's economy by cutting the shipping costs between western farmers and eastern city dwellers. After a long and heated debate, the legislature granted the huge sum of $6 million, and construction began in the summer of 1817.

Few American engineers were experienced in canal building, so the crews had to learn as they worked. They soon developed inventions such as a huge two-wheeled device that pulled trees from the ground, roots and all, and a special cement that hardened even under water. For seven years the crews worked, often under pelting rains or a torrid sun. Finally, miraculously, the project was completed.

While bands played and cannons boomed, De Witt Clinton officially opened the Erie Canal on October 26, 1825. It ran 363 miles (584 kilometers) from Albany on the Hudson River to Buffalo on the shores of Lake Erie. The waterway was 40 feet (12 meters) wide and 4 feet (1.2 meters) deep. A series of ingeniously designed locks lifted canal barges over the foothills of the Appalachian Mountains. The barges were towed by teams of horses or mules that trudged over a towpath next to the canal.

The canal was an immediate success. Tolls paid by barge owners quickly returned the state's construction costs. Most important, the canal helped settle the American Midwest, because it allowed

**New York governor DeWitt Clinton was the moving force behind construction of
the Erie Canal, which opened in 1825 and helped settle the American Midwest.**

farm families to ride barges to Lake Erie, instead of going by the
exhausting and dangerous overland routes. The travelers then
transferred to lake ships for the voyage to Illinois, Wisconsin,
Michigan, and other burgeoning new states.

New businesses and a fresh way of life developed in canal
towns such as Rexford, Schenectady, Fonda, Little Falls, Seneca
Falls, Medina, and Lockport. Feed stores, hotels, and restaurants
in these towns serviced the slow-moving barges and their crews.
In the twilight that marked the end of a long workday,
townspeople often heard crew members sing this lively song:

> I've got a mule and her name is Sal,
> Fifteen years on the Erie Canal.
> She's a good old worker and a good old pal,
> Fifteen years on the Erie Canal.
> We've hauled some barges in our day,
> Filled with lumber, coal, and hay,
> And we know every inch of the way
> From Albany to Buffalo.

In August 1807, Robert Fulton's steamboat, the *Clermont*, traveled up the Hudson River from New York to Albany.

INDUSTRIES AND HUMAN RIGHTS

New York's first railroad, chartered in 1826, connected Albany with Schenectady. Soon, another railroad crossed the width of the state to link Albany with Buffalo. Robert Fulton's first commercially successful steamboat, the *Clermont*, made its initial run in 1807. The idea of operating a steamboat seemed radical, so the *Clermont* was called "Fulton's Folly." But forty years later, at least one hundred steamboats plied the Hudson River alone. Early steamboats averaged five miles (eight kilometers) an hour, and sounded, according to one report, "like a devil in a sawmill."

In the first half of the nineteenth century, New York became a breeding ground for millionaires. John Jacob Astor made a fortune in the West Coast fur trade and invested his money in New York City real estate. He became one of the wealthiest men in the world, and Astor family members dominated New York's high society for generations to come. Cornelius Vanderbilt, who started out as the captain of a Staten Island ferryboat, gradually built the world's leading steamship line. Vanderbilt, Jay Gould, James Fisk, and Daniel Drew made vast fortunes in the railroad industry. Gould was particularly ruthless in his business dealings and was often called the "most hated man in America."

New York politicians and political organizations also grew powerful during the early 1800s. In 1836, Martin Van Buren became the first New Yorker to be elected president of the United States. Van Buren was a member of the "Albany Regency," a group of Democratic party leaders who controlled state government by giving important jobs to political allies. Another political organization called Tammany Hall wielded great, and sometimes corrupt, power in New York City.

While some New Yorkers became wealthy and powerful, others had few rights and were unable to rise from poverty. The struggling groups included landless whites, blacks, and women.

Large New York landowners ruled over their holdings much like feudal lords. Small farmers were allowed to live on and work tiny plots of the large estates, but they had to pay rent to the owners. In some cases, the relationship between landlord and tenant families could be traced back two hundred years. In 1839, farmers in Columbia and Delaware counties refused to pay their rents and the Antirent Wars began. The "wars" were really a series of skirmishes fought between antirent farmers and sheriff's police trying to evict them. The farmers' defiance was rewarded in 1847 when state laws were amended to give tenants the land they had rented for so many years. At about the same time, the state government rescinded a law that said only property owners were allowed to vote.

Slavery in New York existed under the Dutch, the British, and the Americans. At the time of the revolutionary war, about 10 percent of New York's population was black, and most were slaves. Slavery was abolished in New York in 1827. However, blacks could not vote, and they faced discrimination wherever they lived in the state. A French visitor to New York City soundly scolded the city's whites when he wrote: "Are [blacks] outside the

New York-born Elizabeth Cady Stanton (left) led a crusade to win voting privileges for women. It was a long and often unpopular struggle, however (above), and Stanton died before woman suffrage became law.

common law? No. But public prejudice persecutes them more tyranically than any law. They are denied [the horsedrawn buses] and excluded from the churches. That's how these Democrats interpret equality, and these Puritans, Christian charity."

New York women suffered the same discrimination as did their sisters in every other state. They did not have the right to vote, their right to inherit property was limited, most were denied a college education, and professions such as law and medicine were virtually closed to them. The first step to correct these abuses was taken in New York. In the tiny town of Seneca Falls, a convention run by women met in 1848 and issued a famous declaration, "The history of mankind is a history of repeated injuries and usurpations on the part of men toward women . . . ." One of the convention members was New York-born Elizabeth Cady Stanton. She led a crusade to win voting privileges for women but died before woman suffrage became law.

During the draft riots of 1863, Union troops were pulled off the battlefield at Gettysburg to help put down the disturbance. These troops of the Fifth U.S. Artillery were on duty in City Hall Park during the riot.

THE CIVIL WAR

The war between the North and the South exploded in 1861. Although no battles were fought on New York soil, the nation's worst civilian disturbance rocked New York City as mobs rioted against the military draft. For three chaotic days during the summer of 1863, mobs swarmed through the streets, looting stores and burning buildings. Because the Civil War was fought over the issue of slavery, the rioters channeled their rage toward blacks. Innocent blacks were hanged or beaten to death. An orphan home built to house black children was burned to the ground. Union troops had to be pulled off the battlefield at Gettysburg to quell the disturbance. Before order was restored, more than twelve hundred people had been killed and ten times that many injured.

Despite the savagery of the draft riots, New York was a keystone to the Union's victory. Its farms contributed wheat and its factories guns and ships. Half a million New Yorkers—a greater number than from any other state—served in the Union ranks. About fifty thousand of those soldiers died on far-flung battlefields.

The dynamic industrial expansion that occurred after the Civil War created a need for improved transportation. Railroads spread from town to town throughout the country, and cities such as New York built streetcar and elevated tracks.

THE CONFIDENT YEARS

After the Civil War, New York enjoyed dynamic industrial expansion. In New York City, Isaac Singer's factories churned out thousands of sewing machines. In Yonkers, Elisha Graves Otis invented a practical elevator and started a company that built electric elevators for high-rise buildings. In Troy, a factory owned by Henry Burden produced an amazing thirty-six hundred horseshoes an hour. Steel plants grew in Buffalo, and glass-producing factories rose in Corning. Railroads spread to every country hamlet, and in New York City, streetcar tracks ran from City Hall to the newly opened Central Park.

New York's booming industries required the skills and muscles of workers. Beginning in the 1880s, newcomers of a different breed began to land on New York's shores. They came from southern and eastern Europe. Many were Catholic. Many were Jewish. Yankees and other old-line New Yorkers shook their heads in disgust as they saw these alien hordes jam their cities. Still the immigrants came—by the thousands.

Political scandals tarnished the confident years. Tammany Hall's William Marcy "Boss" Tweed gained control of New York City's government, and his power spread throughout the state. Tweed won the support of poor immigrants by doling out government jobs to the few and making empty promises to the many. Before he was exposed and jailed in the early 1870s, Tweed and his henchmen stole nearly $200 million in state funds. But the Tweed experience woke up New Yorkers, and they elected a series of capable governors. One of them was Grover Cleveland, who later became president of the United States.

Toward the turn of the century, the surge of industry and the parade of state millionaires continued in full force. In Rochester, a bank clerk named George Eastman developed an affordable hand-held camera, and soon half the country was snapping pictures on "Eastman Kodaks." The greatest empire builder of all was John D. Rockefeller, who established the giant Standard Oil Company and became the world's wealthiest man.

The crowning glory of the confident years was the completion of the Statue of Liberty, a gift from France. When she was unveiled in 1886, the lovely lady gazed over New York harbor and welcomed the flood of immigrants that arrived daily. To impoverished Europeans, she was the beacon of a new nation. She also represented the coming of a new age, for Lady Liberty not only looked toward the Atlantic Ocean—she faced the twentieth century.

Chapter 6

INTO THE TWENTIETH CENTURY

INTO THE TWENTIETH CENTURY

Almost in the shadow of the Statue of Liberty lies tiny, rock-strewn Ellis Island. In 1892, an enormous immigrant processing center was built there, and by 1932, twelve million people had passed through its halls. Today it is estimated that one of three Americans has a close relative who entered the country through Ellis Island.

THE HUDDLED MASSES

A large number of immigrants looked upon New York as their journey's end and stayed in the state. The 1930 census revealed that more than half of all New Yorkers were either foreign-born or had foreign-born parents.

The greatest of all multicultural cities was New York. On a summer day, a person could tell the character of a neighborhood simply by taking a deep breath and determining whether the cooking smells were Hungarian, Italian, Greek, or Polish. An exciting life flourished in ethnically mixed neighborhoods such as Manhattan's Lower East Side. Pushcarts jammed the avenues and vendors sold everything from shoes to sauerkraut.

The world of New York City's immigrants was one of toil and poverty. As many as five hundred people lived in some three-story tenement buildings. Four or five families shared a single bathroom. Children as young as ten labored at piecework sewing

The millions of immigrants who came to America during the late 1800s and early 1900s passed through Ellis Island (left, bottom left, bottom right). A large number of those immigrants started their new lives in bustling, vibrant neighborhoods such as Manhattan's Lower East Side (above). Most of them were forced by poverty to live in crowded tenements (below).

Child labor (right) contributed to New York's amazing industrial progress during the early 1900s, when New Yorker Theodore Roosevelt (above) was president.

for the garment industry. One of the city's worst tragedies occurred in 1911 when the Triangle Shirtwaist Factory building burned down, killing 146 workers, most of them young Jewish girls newly arrived from Europe. Gradually, through hard work, many immigrants broke the bonds of poverty and saw their children become doctors, lawyers, or teachers.

THE IMPERIAL CITY

The period before World War I saw amazing progress throughout the state. New industries rose and bridges and roadways were built or improved. New Yorker Theodore Roosevelt served as president of the United States from 1901 to 1909. And New York City expanded as if it knew no limits.

Modern New York was formed in 1898 when Manhattan united with the communities of Brooklyn, Queens, the Bronx, and Staten Island. Previously, New York City had been confined to Manhattan. The marriage of the boroughs increased the city's area tenfold and almost doubled its population. With 3.5 million people, Greater New York was the world's second-largest city. Only London eclipsed it.

The union of Manhattan with Brooklyn, Queens, the Bronx, and Staten Island in 1898 to form modern New York would not have worked had the city not improved transportation by connecting the boroughs with bridges, subways, and underground tunnels.

Improved transportation between boroughs was the key to their political union. The breathtaking Brooklyn Bridge opened in 1883, allowing traffic between Brooklyn and Manhattan. By 1910, the Manhattan and Williamsburg bridges also linked Manhattan to Brooklyn, and the Queensborough Bridge connected Queens to Manhattan. The city's first subway opened in 1904. With the completion of underwater tunnels, subway lines soon ran to all the city's boroughs except Staten Island. Electric trolley cars rumbled over the main streets. Brooklynites, who had to scamper out of the way of the swift-moving streetcars, called themselves "trolley-dodgers." Brooklyn's popular baseball team later took that name.

Giant corporations raced each other to establish headquarters in Manhattan. John D. Rockefeller and steel tycoon Andrew Carnegie placed their central offices in Manhattan's financial district. They were followed by insurance companies, publishers, banks, and law firms. The New York Stock Exchange, at Broad and Wall streets, traded millions of dollars worth of shares each day. The great canyons of office buildings that so characterize Manhattan today began to rise early in the twentieth century.

BOOM AND BUST

Alfred E. Smith was born in New York City's Lower East Side
slums. He dropped out of school at age twelve and worked as a
newsboy and a fish seller. He was elected governor in 1919 and
served four terms in that office. Though he was a product of the
city's notorious Tammany Hall, Smith brought honest and
effective government to Albany. The Democratic party chose him
to be its presidential candidate in 1928, but he was defeated by
Herbert Hoover. Smith was the first Roman Catholic to make a
serious run for the presidency, and many historians believe
American voters rejected him because of his religion. Another
1920s member of Tammany Hall was New York City's mayor,
Jimmy Walker. A fun-loving former songwriter, Walker was a
frequent customer in Broadway nightclubs. But while the mayor
partied, his associates raided the city treasury, and Walker was
forced to resign from office in disgrace.

The 1920s was a time of roaring music, gaudy entertainment,
and what seemed to be perpetual prosperity. Then the bubble
burst.

October 24, 1929, began as a normal day on New York City's
Wall Street. True, the stock market had been faltering for a month,
but investors were confident that it would recover. That morning,
however, the price of shares on the New York Stock Exchange
tumbled. Investors panicked and began a tidal wave of selling. By
the end of the day, shares on the exchange had declined by
$8 billion. In only a few hours, thousands of people had lost the
savings of a lifetime.

Largely because of the stock-market crash, the prosperity of the
1920s gave way to the Great Depression of the 1930s. Bank
failures, massive unemployment, and worldwide poverty followed

During the depths of the Great Depression, thousands of jobless families lived in makeshift communities such as this one in Central Park (left). Many stood in long bread lines to get something to eat (above).

Wall Street's collapse. In New York and elsewhere, factories ground to a halt and farmers found only meager prices for their produce.

During the depths of the Great Depression, Americans elected New York's governor Franklin Delano Roosevelt to be their president. A distant cousin of Theodore Roosevelt and a member of an old Hudson River family, Roosevelt launched what he called the "New Deal." He set in motion public works such as road and bridge building that were designed to create jobs for unemployed workers. As governor, Roosevelt had begun this form of depression relief in New York, and in the White House, he extended it to the rest of the country. Although the effects of the depression lingered, Roosevelt's New Deal gave the country fresh hope.

In New York City, Fiorello Henry LaGuardia, the son of an Italian immigrant, became mayor in 1933 and served for twelve years. To city residents, he was a man of many faces. He was flamboyant. To dramatize his war on crime, LaGuardia took axe in hand and helped to chop up a pile of illegal slot machines. He

Despite the depression, several major projects were completed in New York, including the Empire State Building (left) and Rockefeller Center (above).

was exciting. When the fire bells rang, LaGuardia hopped on the back of a fire truck and sped to the blaze. He was warm and funny. During a newspaper strike, LaGuardia volunteered to read the Sunday comics over the radio to the city's children. At one point during the reading, he said, "Look at Dick Tracy. He's always so slim. Chief, why is it our detectives get so fat?"

Despite the depression, several exciting projects were completed in New York City. The Empire State Building—at the time the world's tallest building—was capped off in 1931. The graceful complex of buildings known as Rockefeller Center also rose, and the New York World's Fair opened at Flushing Meadows in 1939.

THE WAR AND POSTWAR PERIOD

The demands of World War II jolted New York out of the Great Depression. Buffalo became a major aircraft producer. Rochester provided photographic equipment and bombsights. The Port of New York shipped half the troops and a third of the supplies destined for fighting fronts in Europe and Africa. But, as always, wartime prosperity came with a tragic price tag. Thousands of New Yorkers died while serving their country.

During the war years, many blacks and Puerto Ricans moved to New York seeking industrial jobs. They discovered that most factories refused to hire minorities for anything but the most menial tasks and that decent housing was frequently closed to them. Blacks coming to New York City were forced to live either in Harlem or in Brooklyn's Bedford-Stuyvesant section, both of which became overcrowded slums. Puerto Ricans found housing in East Harlem, where tenement apartments bulged with people.

At war's end, New York City became a world capital when the newly formed United Nations (UN) established its headquarters there. The glass-and-steel UN building was built on an eighteen-acre (seven-hectare) site donated by the Rockefeller family. New York launched ambitious postwar projects to clear slums and build highways. Directing the program was city planner Robert Moses. While some New Yorkers hailed Moses as a genius, others complained that he concentrated on grandiose projects while letting everyday facilities, such as the subway, decline.

On the potato fields of Long Island, a new community called Levittown sprang to life. A town totally dependent on automobiles for transportation, Levittown is considered to be the first modern suburb. While the look-alike houses appeared monotonous, they could be purchased by newly discharged war veterans for $60 monthly payments. But Levittown was off-limits to nonwhites. A clause in each home buyer's contract read, "The buyer agrees not to permit the premises to be used or occupied by any person other than members of the Caucasian race."

The postwar years saw a radical population shift in New York City as more blacks and Puerto Ricans moved in and whites fled

Among Governor Nelson A. Rockefeller's pet projects were the Empire State Plaza in Albany (left) and the Lincoln Center complex in New York City (above).

to the suburbs. The 1960 census revealed that during the previous decade, more than a million middle-class whites had left the city.

Despite the shifting population, a positive spirit spread through the Big Apple in the 1950s and early 1960s. The business community was so confident in the city's future that investors tore down thirty-story office buildings and replaced them with fifty-story structures. New Yorkers even laughed at crises. In 1965, a sudden power failure blacked out most of the city. Passengers were trapped for hours in pitch-dark elevators and subway trains, but few people panicked. In fact, in some subway cars, the stranded passengers sang songs.

FINANCES AND FRUSTRATIONS

Nelson A. Rockefeller, grandson of the founder of Standard Oil, was elected governor in 1958 and served for fifteen years. Under his direction, superhighways were built on Long Island, along the southern part of the state (the southern tier), and across the Adirondack Mountains. The futuristic buildings of the Albany Mall and New York City's Lincoln Center were among his pet projects. He pursued building programs with such zeal that one journalist suggested that Rockefeller had "changed the physical face of New York more than any governor since De Witt Clinton built the Erie Canal."

Largely due to Rockefeller's enterprises, the cost of state government zoomed from $2 billion during his first year in office to $8.8 billion in his last year. Critics denounced Rockefeller's habit of putting off debt payments "until tomorrow." In 1974, newly elected governor Hugh Carey announced, "To the citizens of New York, I say: Tomorrow is here." To pay back the state's debts, Carey had to increase taxes and cut back spending.

New York City also suffered a financial crisis brought about by overspending. The municipal budget doubled between 1965 and 1973, and by 1975 the city was all but bankrupt. Though the federal and state governments came to the rescue, New York City was forced to cut thousands of people from its payroll. Because he was blamed for the financial plight, Mayor John Lindsay was compelled to give up a promising political career.

The late 1960s and early 1970s were angry years in New York and in the rest of the nation. New York City suffered a series of crippling strikes by garbage collectors, police, fire fighters, and transit workers. Racial disorders rocked black neighborhoods. The state's worst riot broke out in 1971 when inmates at Attica Prison rebelled. Before order was restored, thirty-three prisoners and ten members of the prison staff had been killed.

Street crime became the most talked-about issue in New York City. Though New York's crime rate was no worse than that of other large cities, horror stories about the mean streets flourished. Many of the street criminals were drug addicts. Dangerous drugs such as heroin and cocaine, which were once confined to the slums, had pushed into nearly every neighborhood.

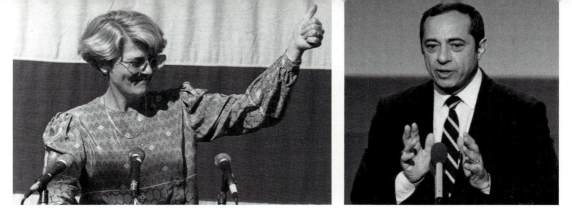

Geraldine Ferraro was the 1984 Democratic nominee for vice-president and Governor Mario Cuomo gave a stirring Democratic convention keynote speech.

New York City suffered another power blackout in 1977, and this crisis demonstrated how the Big Apple had changed. New York City residents had turned their first power failure into a celebration, but the second one was a nightmare. Within thirty minutes after the lights went out, looters had smashed hundreds of store windows and had run off with $150 million in goods.

TODAY'S NEW YORK

Major newsmakers of the 1980s were Governor Mario Cuomo and New York City Mayor Edward Koch. Democrats raved about Cuomo's stirring speech before their national convention in 1984, and many urged Cuomo to run for the presidency. Mayor Koch was a lively figure and was often interviewed on television. Both the mayor and the governor wrote best-selling books.

In 1984, the Democratic party nominated Queens congresswoman Geraldine Ferraro to be their vice-presidential candidate. She was the first woman named by a major party to run for national office. Twelve years earlier, Brooklyn congresswoman Shirley Chisholm had been the first woman and the first black to launch a serious campaign for president.

Racial tension and crime remained heated issues in New York City. In 1984, a slightly built computer specialist named Bernhard

New York City's Wall Street made headlines in October 1987, when the New York Stock Exchange took a disastrous plunge.

Goetz shot and wounded four black teenagers who, he claimed, were trying to rob him. The youths later said they were merely begging for money. Some New Yorkers called Goetz a racist criminal, while others praised him for defending himself. The shootings made headlines as far away as Tokyo and London. A jury later found that Goetz had fired in self-defense and convicted him only for carrying a gun.

New York City's Wall Street commanded world attention in October 1987, when the New York Stock Exchange took a disastrous one-day plunge. Wall Street's collapse triggered a sharp downturn of stocks in Tokyo, Hong Kong, Sydney, and London. This international chain reaction confirmed an old saying, "When Wall Street sneezes, the rest of the world catches a cold."

The world celebrated the one hundredth birthday of the Statue of Liberty in 1986. Scores of dignitaries, including President Ronald Reagan and French President Francois Mitterrand, attended the gala event. Brass bands played and tons of fireworks lit the night sky. Lady Liberty had never looked so grand as she once again reminded the world that New York is still America's golden gateway.

Chapter 7

GOVERNMENT AND THE ECONOMY

GOVERNMENT AND THE ECONOMY

If New York were an independent nation, it would be one of the richest, most productive countries on earth. To keep its vast enterprises running smoothly requires close cooperation between state government and the business community.

GOVERNMENT

New York's constitution divides state government into three branches: the executive, the legislative, and the judicial. The executive branch is headed by the governor, and its function is to enforce laws. The legislative branch consists of two houses: a 61-member senate and a 150-member assembly. The legislature creates new laws and rescinds old ones. The judicial branch, which is the court system, interprets laws and tries cases.

The governor of New York is elected to a four-year term and may be reelected to an unlimited number of terms. The governor's broad powers include the authority to appoint key persons to government posts and to call out the state militia in cases of emergency. Other important executive officers—all of whom are elected to four-year terms—include the lieutenant governor, the attorney general, and the comptroller.

Members of the senate and the assembly are elected to two-year terms. Legislators debate proposed laws, called bills. When both houses agree on the details of a bill, it is sent to the governor. The governor's signature makes a bill a law. The governor can reject, or veto, a bill, but the legislature can override that veto with sufficient votes.

Preparing the annual budget is the state's stormiest issue. A typical one-year budget in the 1980s was more than $32 billion—more than most independent nations spend. To raise money, New York relies on grants from the federal government, a sales tax, an income tax, a corporate tax, and taxes on alcohol, tobacco, and gasoline. Since 1967, New York has sponsored a state lottery, the profits of which go to the public schools.

New York's highest court is the court of appeals, made up of a chief justice and six associate justices. Judges on the court of appeals are elected to fourteen-year terms. The court system tries cases that range from criminal offenses to business disagreements.

The center of local government is the county. Within the state's sixty-two counties are village, town, and city governments. The form local government takes varies from one community to another. Local governments provide services such as community colleges, police forces, and street and park maintenance. New York City's government is enormous. Its annual budget is greater than that of some American states, and its police force is the size of many foreign armies.

EDUCATION

Since 1784, a sixteen-member Board of Regents has directed the state school system. The system embraces 735 local school districts. State law directs that children from ages six through sixteen must attend school. It costs the state nearly $5,000 per year to educate each student. This is the highest per-student expenditure of any state except Alaska.

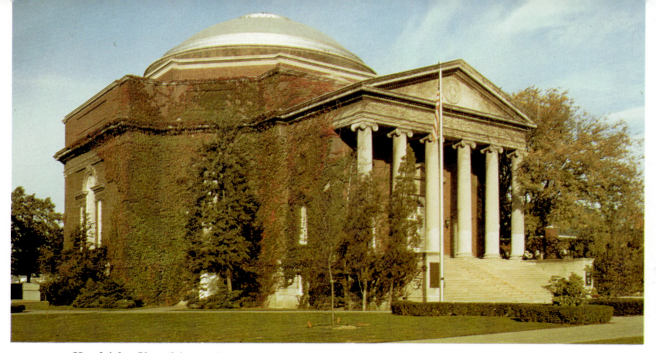

Hendricks Chapel is on the campus of Syracuse University, one of
New York State's most prestigious privately funded universities.

About 16 percent of elementary and secondary students attend
nonpublic schools. Most of the private schools are church
affiliated; the Roman Catholic system is the largest. Private-school
attendance is highest in Albany, with 39 percent, and lowest in
Jamestown, with 5.6 percent.

New York has many outstanding private and publicly funded
colleges and universities. The tax-supported State University of
New York, headquartered in Albany, runs seventy colleges and
specialized schools throughout the state. The State University of
New York is one of the country's largest networks of colleges.
Some of the state's most prestigious privately funded colleges
include Cornell University in Ithaca; Colgate University in
Hamilton; Vassar College in Poughkeepsie; Columbia University,
New York University, St. John's University, and Fordham
University, all in New York City; Utica College, Niagara
University, Syracuse University, and the University of Rochester.

Milk from dairy farms such as this one in Bloomfield and cherries from Hudson Valley orchards are among New York State's important agricultural products.

AGRICULTURE

New York has about forty-nine thousand farms, which average 201 acres (81.3 hectares) in size. The state is second only to Wisconsin in milk production and income from dairy products. It ranks first in producing cream cheese and cottage cheese.

New York City residents' demand for fresh vegetables has spurred the development of large upstate truck farms. (Truck farms specialize in raising produce for a nearby market.) New York truck farms grow beets, sweet corn, potatoes, carrots, cauliflower, and celery. New York is the nation's third-largest producer of cabbage and snap beans.

Fruit grows especially well along the flatlands on Lake Erie's shore. The lakeside city of Dunkirk calls itself the "Concord Grape Capital of the World." Only California produces more grapes for wine than does New York. New York also produces huge crops of cherries and apples.

Livestock farmers raise beef cattle, hogs, and sheep. The state ranks third in the production of clover and alfalfa. Each year, almost 2 billion eggs and 9 million chickens come from New York farms. One of four of the nation's ducks is raised on Long Island.

New York City's Wall Street area has been a financial center since the country's beginnings. The twin towers of the nearby World Trade Center (left) house dozens of corporate headquarters.

BANKING AND FINANCE

Almost half a million people work in New York City's banks, brokerage houses, and insurance companies. The New York Stock Exchange (the world's largest) and the American Stock Exchange are the heart of the city's financial district. The Wall Street area has been a financial center since the country's beginnings. Shares exchanged there helped finance the American Revolution.

One of five of America's five hundred largest companies have headquarters in New York City. Some of these corporate giants are RCA, Woolworth, and Mobil. To house the many financial headquarters, the city put up more new office buildings in the postwar era than did Chicago, Los Angeles, and San Francisco combined. The city's tallest structure—the twin-towered World Trade Center—contains dozens of corporate headquarters.

Though foreign competition has cut into New York City's clothing business, apparel is still designed, manufactured, and traded in the city's garment district.

MANUFACTURING

New York ranks second, behind California, as the nation's leading manufacturing state. Plants turn out everything from toys for babies to diesel engines the size of a house.

Buffalo and its suburbs have steel mills and automobile assembly plants. Rochester makes photographic equipment and office copying machines. The General Electric Company dominates Utica and Schenectady. Food processing is a major business in Niagara Falls. Syracuse produces electric machinery. Computers are made in the tri-city area of Binghamton, Endicott, and Johnson City. Printing—the state's largest industry—is centered in the New York City area. The city once housed an enormous clothing industry that employed generations of immigrants. Foreign competition has cut into the clothing business, but apparel is still traded in the city's garment district.

MINING AND NATURAL RESOURCES

New York's leading minerals are stone, sand and gravel, and gypsum—all of which are vital materials for the construction industry. Emery, which is used to make grinding wheels, is mined in Westchester County. The southern tier provides oil and natural gas.

Lumber companies harvest birch, cherry, maple, spruce, and white pine trees. Logging is a carefully controlled industry, and most New York companies plant more trees than they cut down. Commercial fishing takes place along Long Island and in Lake Erie and Lake Ontario. Clams, lobsters, oysters, flounder, and scallops are taken from the Atlantic Ocean, while walleye and perch are caught in the two Great Lakes.

TRANSPORTATION

New York's network of roads includes the New York State (Thomas E. Dewey) Thruway, a major highway that crosses the state from New York City to the northwest tip of Pennsylvania. In the 1970s and 1980s, when railroading experienced a decline, the state government had to take over several New York City commuter lines to preserve the service. The longest waterway is the New York State Barge Canal, which was completed in 1918 and incorporates much of the old Erie Canal. New York is an important link on the St. Lawrence Seaway, which allows oceangoing ships to enter the Great Lakes. About five hundred airports operate within the state. John F. Kennedy Airport handles more international flights than any other airfield in the nation.

New York City has long depended on bridges and tunnels to meet its transportation needs. Manhattan Island alone is served by

About twelve hundred ships dock at New York City each year, making it one of the world's most important seaports.

twenty bridges and twenty-two tunnels. The Brooklyn Bridge, the grandfather of the large bridges, accommodates one hundred thousand automobiles each working day. The Verrazano-Narrows Bridge, which links Brooklyn and Staten Island, is the world's second-largest suspension bridge. The George Washington Bridge, between Manhattan and New Jersey, is the fourth largest. The Holland Tunnel lies 100 feet (30.4 meters) below the Hudson River. The Lincoln Tunnel is said to be the world's busiest tunnel.

New York City remains one of the world's most important seaports. About twelve hundred ships dock there each year, and the port employs two hundred thousand people. Docking facilities are regulated by a gigantic government agency called the Port of New York Authority. The Port Authority's sweeping powers include the administration of four major airports, two heliports, and the always-jammed bus station near Times Square. Great

Lakes and Seaway ports include Buffalo, Oswego, Rochester, and Ogdensburg. Though Albany lies 150 miles (241 kilometers) from the Atlantic Ocean, dredging of the Hudson River allows the city to receive oceangoing ships.

The New York City subway system is the world's largest. About 3.5 million people ride its trains each working day.

COMMUNICATIONS

New York publishes 90 daily newspapers and 750 weeklies. The *New York Times* is hailed as one of the world's most prestigious newspapers. With two million readers, the *New York Daily News* enjoys the nation's highest circulation. The financial world's "bible," the *Wall Street Journal*, is published in New York City. The city also boasts two lively Spanish-language newspapers, *El Diario-La Prensa* and *El Tiempo*. The *Amsterdam News* is the city's leading black-oriented newspaper. Russian-, Polish-, Greek-, and Chinese-language papers also circulate in the big city. Major book publishers and popular magazines such as *Time*, *Life*, and *Newsweek* have their headquarters in the Big Apple.

New York City is the nation's television capital. The three major networks—NBC, ABC, and CBS—all have headquarters there. The city is also home to the Mutual Broadcasting System, the country's largest radio network. Statewide, New York has forty television stations and more than three hundred radio stations.

THE ENVIRONMENT

Industrialization brings jobs and prosperity, but often at a high cost. While the state's factories have thrived, the quality of its environment has declined.

Centuries ago, the Algonquian people simply dipped their cups into the Hudson River when they wanted to drink. Today, most of the fish that swim in the southern portion of that river are diseased. Refuse from paper mills, chemical plants, and city sewers has fouled the once-clear Hudson. Great Moose Lake in the Adirondacks still sparkles like diamonds in the sunset, but it and neighboring lakes have been ravaged by acid rain. A bed of autumn leaves covers the bottom of many Adirondack lakes because the waters lack the bacteria to dissolve them. In 1978, people living near Niagara Falls were forced to evacuate their homes because toxic chemicals had been illegally dumped years earlier at Love Canal, and poisonous muck was seeping into their basements.

Air pollution and garbage are New York City's primary environmental headaches. The millions of cars and trucks choking city streets emit fumes that burn the throat and sting the eyes. During summertime smog alerts, people with heart or bronchial problems are urged to stay indoors. New York City dwellers throw away 23,000 tons (20,865 metric tons) of rubbish each day—so much that city officials have run out of places to put it. In 1987, a garbage barge left New York harbor on a routine dumping mission that turned into a five-month odyssey. A dozen states and three foreign countries refused to allow the barge to deposit New York's mess into their landfill areas. Finally, a judge permitted engineers to burn the decaying trash.

However, New York is making great strides to protect its environment. Beginning in the 1960s, laws were tightened to restrict the dumping of industrial waste into the state's rivers. A recent series of tests determined that the cleanup campaign has worked. The Hudson River near New York City will be opened for swimming in the early 1990s.

Chapter 8

ARTS AND ENTERTAINMENT

ARTS AND ENTERTAINMENT

New Yorkers insist that their state is the cultural front-runner of the nation. To prove the contention, they cite a golden honor roll of artists, writers, and entertainers who have lived and worked in the Empire State.

THE FINE ARTS

New York painters burst into American art history with the formation of the Hudson River school—a loose fraternity of artists who worked from the 1820s through the 1870s. The painters brought the dramatic world of nature to their canvases. The stunningly beautiful Hudson River Valley was their favorite workplace. Founder of the movement was English-born Thomas Cole. Cole and his followers broke with the European tradition of painting gentle outdoor landscapes, and instead portrayed the power of a thunderstorm breaking over a mountaintop or the surging grandeur of a waterfall.

New York City resident Winslow Homer was one of America's most beloved painters of the post-Civil War era. He admired fishermen and sailors and portrayed these workers going about their daily tasks with great dignity.

In the late 1800s, newspaper cartoonist Thomas Nast published biting satirical drawings of political figures. His cartoons helped put Tammany Hall's "Boss" Tweed in jail. Nast is also credited

Eight Bells, by artist Winslow Homer, shows one of his favorite subjects—men of the sea concentrating on their daily tasks.

with creating the modern image of Santa Claus. Jacob Riis used photography as a tool of social protest by venturing into New York City's slums and shooting pictures of the conditions he found there. Riis's 1890 book, *How the Other Half Lives,* shocked middle-class Americans.

Near the end of the nineteenth century, a group of New York City artists painted the seedy side of life by setting up easels in poolrooms and saloons. Some critics called them the New York City Realists; others dubbed the group the Ashcan School. The leader of the movement was Robert Henri, whose book *The Art Spirit* is still read by art students.

Artist Jackson Pollock, a member of the New York City Art Students' League, rendered abstract paintings such as this one with bold and splashing colors.

Art movements took place throughout the state in the twentieth century. A colony of artists left New York City in the early 1900s to settle in the Catskill Mountain town of Woodstock. In the 1920s and 1930s, art colonies appeared in Oyster Bay, Saratoga Springs, and Buffalo. In New York City, the Art Students' League blossomed.

Edward Hopper was one of New York's most important modern painters. Hopper was born in Nyack, New York, and lived in New York City. On canvas he captured the loneliness and isolation of big-city life. His famous painting *Nighthawks* shows men and women brooding over coffee cups in an all-night cafe. Jackson Pollock, a longtime member of the Art Students' League, rendered abstract paintings with bold and splashing colors.

Washington Irving (far left) and James Fenimore Cooper (left) were two of New York's best-known writers.

LITERATURE

Washington Irving, who lived in Tarrytown, based his lively short stories "Rip Van Winkle" and "The Legend of Sleepy Hollow" on Dutch folktales. He ridiculed the Dutch in his satirical book usually known as *Knickerbocker's History of New York* (knickerbockers were the bloused trousers worn by Dutch patroons). James Fenimore Cooper drew on Indian legends in his books *The Deerslayer* and *The Last of the Mohicans*.

Today, Herman Melville is recognized as one of America's greatest novelists, but he spent most of his adult life working as a low-paid customs inspector for the Port of New York. As a writer, his popularity peaked just before he published his masterpiece, *Moby Dick*, the story of a sea captain obsessed with killing a great white whale.

Poet Walt Whitman was born near Huntington, Long Island, and grew up in Brooklyn. He was a religious mystic who believed the journey of the soul included birth, life, death, and rebirth. Whitman championed American democracy, and after President Lincoln's assassination, he wrote one of his most famous poems:

> O Captain! my Captain! our fearful trip is done,
> The ship has weathered every rack, the prize we
> sought is won . . . .

Early in the twentieth century, New York City became the undisputed capital of American literature. The Greenwich Village neighborhood especially was a gathering place for writers. While Damon Runyon was a sportswriter for the *New York American*, he created hilarious short stories about New York City lowlifes. To this day, racetrack followers and chronically broke gamblers are called Runyonesque characters.

Eugene O'Neill was one of America's greatest playwrights. Characters in plays such as *The Iceman Cometh* seek, but usually fail to find, substantial meaning in life. Arthur Miller, who was born in Manhattan, stunned audiences with his powerful 1949 drama *Death of a Salesman*. The work portrayed the step-by-step deterioration of a family, and it censured American greed for material things.

Black writers commanded New York's attention in the years immediately following World War II. In his 1952 book *Invisible Man*, Ralph Ellison told the plight of a New York City black man trapped in the slums, "People refuse to see me . . . . When they approach me they see only my surroundings." Harlem-born James Baldwin cried out with an anguished voice in his 1961 book *Nobody Knows My Name*. Claude Brown's shocking 1965 autobiography, *Manchild in the Promised Land*, told how the introduction of heroin disrupted Harlem life.

New Yorker Isaac Bashevis Singer, who writes the first draft of all his books in Yiddish, received the 1978 Nobel Prize in literature. Among his many works, Singer has written children's books. When asked why he likes to write for young readers, Singer replied, "Because children don't read reviews." In 1984, William Kennedy's novel *Ironweed*, which completed a trilogy that was set in Albany, won both the Pulitzer Prize in fiction and the National Book Critics Circle Award in fiction.

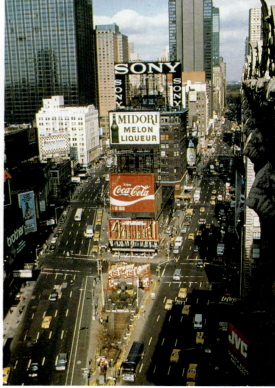

At the Times Square theater district of New York City (right), Broadway becomes the Great White Way, with a sea of theater marquee lights, neon restaurant signs, and signs advertising a multitude of products.

THE MUSIC SCENE

Running the length of Manhattan is the fabulous avenue called Broadway. Early in this century, songwriters such as Irving Berlin, Con Conrad, and George M. Cohan put together Broadway's famous musical shows. Starring in the productions were such singer-comedians as Eddie Cantor, George Jessel, and Al Jolson. At the Times Square theater district, Broadway becomes the Great White Way, with its thousands of theater marquee lights, neon restaurant signs, flashing signs advertising a multitude of products, and bright streetlights. George M. Cohan gave the avenue its own song, "Give My Regards to Broadway."

One of Broadway's most successful musicals was *Showboat*, written in the 1930s by Jerome Kern and featuring the powerful black singer Paul Robeson. Robeson brought audiences to tears with his rendition of "Ol' Man River." Also in the 1930s,

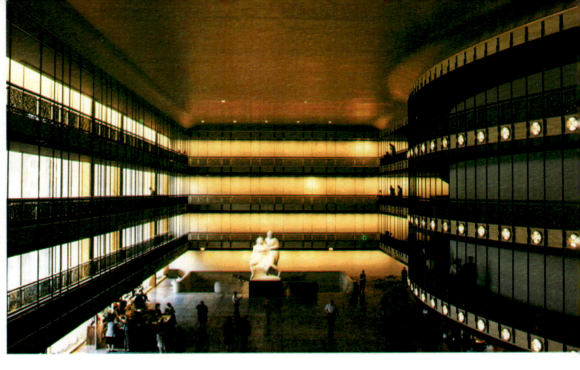

The New York City Ballet, one of the nation's finest dance companies, performs at the New York State Theater (right), which is part of the Lincoln Center complex.

songwriter George Gershwin created his masterpiece *Porgy and Bess*, which many critics claimed rose above the Broadway musical tradition to become fine opera. Early during World War II, the team of Rodgers and Hammerstein produced *Oklahoma!*, perhaps the most popular musical of all time.

The postwar years gave birth to a series of Broadway hits: *My Fair Lady*, *Fiddler on the Roof*, and *A Little Night Music*. But in the 1960s, the cost of musicals and other theatrical productions soared, and dramas were staged in off-Broadway and off-off-Broadway theaters. Some of those smaller theaters were converted from abandoned warehouses.

Classical music lovers flock to the New York Philharmonic Orchestra and the Metropolitan Opera, both of which perform at New York City's Lincoln Center. The New York City Ballet is considered one of the nation's finest dance companies. Students of dance and classical music attend the Juilliard School. During the summer months, classical and jazz concerts are given in the city's Central Park.

Both Babe Ruth (far left) and Lou Gehrig (left), New York Yankee baseball stars of the 1920s, were elected to the National Baseball Hall of Fame.

Important musical organizations upstate include the Buffalo Symphony Orchestra and the Lake George Opera at Glens Falls. The Saratoga Performing Arts Center hosts many great orchestras. The Eastman School of Music, a division of the University of Rochester, is one of America's most prestigious music schools. A major American classical composer, Howard Hanson, directed the Eastman School for many years.

SPORTS

No team in baseball history can match the winning tradition of the New York Yankees. While capturing a record thirty-two American League pennants, the team fielded Babe Ruth and Lou Gehrig in the 1920s, Joe DiMaggio in the 1930s and 1940s, Mickey Mantle and Roger Maris in the 1950s and 1960s, Thurman Munson and Reggie Jackson in the 1970s, and Don Mattingly in the 1980s.

Baseball history and the American conscience were changed forever in 1947 when Brooklyn Dodgers president Branch Rickey made Jackie Robinson the first black major leaguer. In his rookie year, Robinson had to endure vicious racial slurs from many players. But Robinson, Pee Wee Reese, and Duke Snyder headed a mighty team that was later immortalized in sportswriter Roger Kahn's moving book *The Boys of Summer*. The Dodgers' greatest rival was the New York Giants, led by Willie Mays. New York fans still feel betrayed because both the Dodgers and the Giants relocated to the West Coast in 1957. Then the Mets came to town and won World Series crowns in 1969, 1973, and 1986.

Pro football fans follow the Giants and the Jets (both teams are identified with New York but play in the New Jersey Meadowlands), and the Buffalo Bills. Exciting running back O. J. Simpson spent most of his career with the Buffalo Bills. Another former Bills star, Jack Kemp, was elected to Congress from Buffalo and campaigned for the presidency in 1988. The Jets, who fielded their strongest team when led by quarterback Joe Namath, won the Super Bowl in 1969, and the Giants won the Super Bowl in 1987.

A popular sporting event is the annual New York City Marathon—a twenty-six-mile footrace that winds through the streets of the city. The marathon attracts nearly twenty-five thousand runners. The race is made accessible to the handicapped, and wheelchair and blind athletes compete. It took three days for one legless Vietnam veteran to finish the race, but New Yorkers cheered his courage all the way.

In hockey, the Buffalo Sabres, the New York Islanders, and the New York Rangers have legions of devoted fans. Rod Gilbert led the Rangers in the 1960s, and Denis Potvin helped the Islanders win four straight Stanley Cup championships in the early 1980s.

The New York Knickerbockers is the state's professional basketball team. In the early 1970s, the Knicks fielded a strong team led by Willis Reed and Walt Frazier. Bill Bradley, later

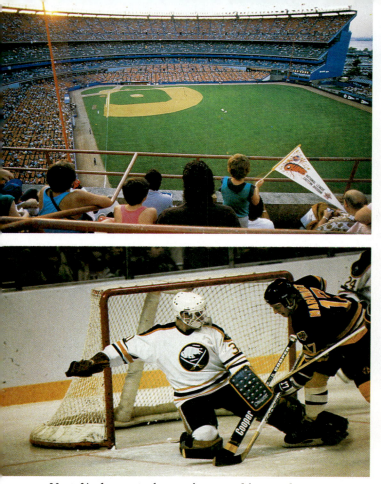

New York sports fans enjoy watching such teams as the Mets (top) and the Buffalo Sabres (above); others enjoy competing in the New York City Marathon (right).

elected to the United States Senate from New Jersey, was a high-scoring forward on that team.

Playground basketball enjoys an almost religious following in New York City's black neighborhoods. A Harlem basketball fan laid bare the community's feelings for the game when he told a sportswriter: "There's a love for the game in this city that is very difficult to put into words. You start off when you're very young and you never get it out of your system. You might get married to a woman, but basketball is still your first love."

Chapter 9

AN UPSTATE TOUR

AN UPSTATE TOUR

It would take a lifetime to see all the attractions upstate New York has to offer, but a brief tour might very well start and end near New York City.

LONG ISLAND AND THE NEW YORK CITY SUBURBS

Long Island is divided into two general regions: the New York City metropolitan area in the west and the rural area in the east.

Eastern Long Island is proud of its past. It was settled almost three hundred years ago by New England farmers and fishermen. In Riverhead, the Suffolk Historical Museum exhibits crafts of the Algonquian people and the Yankee whalers. Nearby Sag Harbor has a whaling museum. The town of Cutchogue boasts a house built on the village green in 1649. Stately old homes are landmarks in Amagansett, East Hampton, and Montauk. On the shore stand windmills that date back to the 1700s. In the distant past, piracy was a thriving business on Long Island. It is believed that notorious buccaneer Captain Kidd buried his treasure on some lonely beach on eastern Long Island, and it supposedly remains there today.

Metropolitan Long Island experienced explosive growth after World War II. In 1945, Nassau County, which lies just beyond the New York City limits, had a population of about 450,000. By 1980, more than 1,300,000 people lived there. But it is a mistake to think

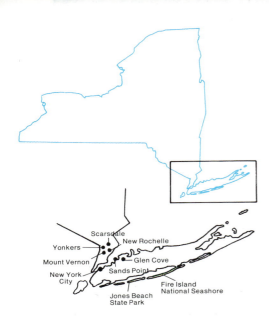

The lighthouse at Fire Island National Seashore

of metropolitan Long Island as a sea of newly built commuter suburbs. The region has miles of ocean beaches and encompasses many towns that were established long before the dynamic suburban expansion.

Jones Beach State Park and Fire Island National Seashore welcome thousands of bathers, strollers, and picnickers. Many travelers claim that Long Island beaches are the finest in the country. At Old Westbury, visitors can tour Old Westbury Gardens—a marvelous mansion surrounded by acres of formal gardens. Mansions are the norm in the towns of Sand Point, Port Washington, Glen Cove, and Mill Neck. But only the very wealthy househunt there. In the late 1980s, the average house in Mill Neck sold for $1.2 million, making it one of the most expensive towns in the nation.

Sag Harbor shops, in eastern Long Island

North of New York City is Westchester County, which contains wealthy towns such as Scarsdale and middle-class suburbs such as Mount Vernon and New Rochelle. Some say that the northern Westchester County border is where New York City's suburbs end and the upstate region begins. The people of Yonkers resent being called suburban because theirs is a self-contained city that has some four hundred manufacturing plants. Thriving industries have made Yonkers the state's fourth-largest city.

THE HUDSON VALLEY

"Nowhere have I ever beheld such a rich and pleasant land," wrote Henry Hudson when he sailed up the river that now bears his name. Today, a leisurely boat cruise is still the best way to see the Hudson Valley. In the southern portion, forest-covered cliffs called palisades rise dramatically from the river's edge. It is this rich scenery that so excited the artists of the Hudson River School.

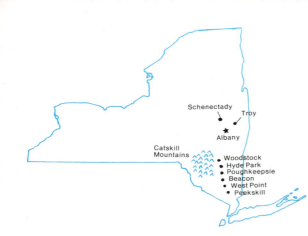

Cadets on the parade ground at the United States Military Academy at West Point

The United States Military Academy at West Point stands at the valley's suburban end. The famous school was founded in 1802 by Thomas Jefferson. Its first class was made up of only ten cadets; today, four thousand future officers study there. Among West Point's distinguished graduates have been Robert E. Lee, Ulysses S. Grant, John Pershing, Douglas MacArthur, and Dwight D. Eisenhower.

The Hudson River town of Peekskill is a success story in race relations. In 1949, a riot broke out when black entertainer Paul Robeson sang there. By 1987, Peekskill had a black mayor.

Farther north, towns and historical sites dot the riverbanks. George Washington's revolutionary war headquarters stands in the city of Newburgh. In Poughkeepsie, Vassar College's art museum holds 8,500 works, including paintings by Hudson River School artists. At Hyde Park, visitors tour the mansion in which President Franklin Roosevelt was born. Upstream is the fifty-four-room mansion once owned by the Vanderbilt family. Both are now museums open to the public.

The Catskill Mountains area (left), west of the Hudson Valley, attracts outdoor lovers. Hyde Park (above), where President Franklin Delano Roosevelt was born, is a Hudson Valley landmark.

To the west, the Catskill Mountains—with dozens of luxury resorts, hotels, motels, and camping sites—is a vacationer's paradise. Hiking, swimming, fishing, golf, and skiing are favorite outdoor sports. In 1969, amid the gloom of the Vietnam War, an incredible "happening" took place at the artists' haven of Woodstock, when 500,000 young people attended a rock concert at a nearby farm. Although drugs passed freely, the Woodstock concert was hailed by many as an almost mystical celebration of peace and love.

At the northern end of the Hudson Valley is the tri-city area of Schenectady, Troy, and Albany. Called the "City that Lights the World" because of the gigantic General Electric plants located there, Schenectady has a natural-history museum, a planetarium, and a fine network of city parks. Troy boasts the interesting Hudson-Mohawk Urban Cultural Park.

The heart of Albany is the capitol building, which resembles a French chateau. Inside, the intricate design of the "million-dollar staircase" is a celebration of the stonecutter's art. The boldly modernistic Empire State Plaza is a broad concourse of government buildings and reflecting pools. Events such as the Great American Music Day, held on July 4, take place there. Also on the plaza is the New York State Museum, where life-sized dioramas tell a chapter-by-chapter history of New York.

Harness racing at Saratoga Springs

THE NORTH

Saratoga Springs is a health spa, a cultural colony, a horse-racing center, and a gathering place for the rich and famous. The Mohawks believed that bathing in this region's mineral-rich springs would cure a whole host of illnesses. In the early 1800s, wealthy New Yorkers journeyed to Saratoga Springs hoping to find renewed health in the waters. The wealthy health seekers brought with them a taste for art and culture. The artists' retreat at Yaddo in Saratoga Springs provides a splendid setting where painters, musicians, and writers can work.

The wildly beautiful Adirondack Mountains cover 5,000 square miles (12,950 square kilometers), making the region larger than most neighboring states. Half the area covered by the mountains is a state park, where hiking trails and canoe routes are endless. The Ausable Chasm invites hikers through a spectacular rock-walled gorge carved out by the Ausable River. Lake Placid—site of the 1932 and 1980 Winter Olympic Games—is one of the Adirondacks' two thousand lakes.

One of the most interesting attractions in the Thousand Islands is Boldt Castle (above and top), on Heart Island, built by millionaire George C. Boldt. Lake Placid (right), one of the two thousand lakes in the Adirondack Mountains, was the site of the 1932 and 1980 Winter Olympics.

In the far north, Lake Champlain stretches for 107 miles (172 kilometers) along the Vermont border. On its western shore, the city of Plattsburgh hosts art exhibits, craft fairs, and summer theater productions. The Thousand Islands—actually there are more than 1,800 of them—dot the St. Lawrence River. Heart Island contains Boldt Castle, built by a New York City millionaire. The Seaway Trail is a scenic route that parallels Lake Ontario's shore and runs past lakeside communities such as Cape Vincent, Watertown, Henderson Harbor, and Pulaski. The port city of Oswego is rich in history. Visitors can tour Fort Ontario (first built in 1755) and see exhibits at the Oswego County Historical Society.

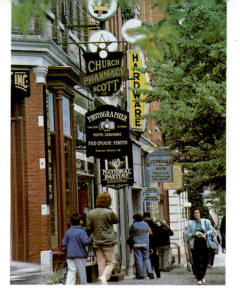

Cooperstown (right), site of the National Baseball Hall of Fame, is also the home of the Farmers' Museum and the New York State Historical Society.

THE MOHAWK VALLEY

The Mohawk Valley begins at Albany and runs westward the width of the state. Along country roads in the valley, a diligent traveler can find sections of the original Erie Canal. In the town of Rome is Erie Canal Village, where people can ride on a replica of a 150-year-old canal barge.

The city of Utica grew around the site of Fort Schuyler. It thrives today due to a diversity of industry. At the city's Children's Museum are many "hands-on" exhibits, and the Italian Culture Center features paintings and sculptures. To the south is Cooperstown, home of the New York State Historical Society, housed in the James Fenimore Cooper mansion, and the Farmers' Museum, a museum honoring James Fenimore Cooper. Cooperstown is also the site of the Baseball Hall of Fame. The Hall of Fame holds more than eight thousand artifacts, including Babe Ruth memorabilia and the earliest known baseball.

Situated in the heart of the Mohawk Valley, Syracuse is the Empire State's fifth-largest city. It has high-tech industrial plants and is the home of Syracuse University and Le Moyne College. Syracuse is also the headquarters of many church groups.

Buffalo City Hall forms a background for a sailboat in the Erie Basin Marina (left). Spectacular Niagara Falls (above) is one of the most famous natural attractions in America.

The series of long, narrow Finger Lakes is a popular vacation area. At Seneca Falls is the Women's Rights National Historical Park, where exhibits trace the struggle for women's liberation.

On the shores of Lake Ontario is Rochester, New York's third-largest city. It is sometimes described as "quiet, conservative, and Kodak." The Eastman Kodak Company, one of the world's largest producers of photographic equipment, employs one out of eleven of the city's workers. The city was founded in 1812 by Nathaniel Rochester and flourished when the Erie Canal was completed.

To the west is the famous Niagara Falls, which draws fifteen million visitors a year. In recent years, Niagara Falls residents have spruced up their city with the addition of a convention center and a glass-enclosed conservatory.

Buffalo, New York's second-largest city, marks the end of the old Erie Canal. It was once one of the nation's greatest factory centers. During World War II, Buffalo's steel production rivaled that of Pittsburgh. But the industrial plants grew old, industry moved elsewhere, and the city lost 22 percent of its population during the 1970s. Yet the people are optimistic about the future. Downtown buildings are being restored rather than bulldozed, new construction projects are underway, and city government is making heroic efforts to attract new businesses.

Two creeks
run through
the beautiful
campus of
Cornell
University,
which overlooks
the city of
Ithaca and
Cayuga Lake.

The Corning Glass Works in the
city of Corning produces fine
decorative glassware (right) as
well as glass used for more
practical purposes. Far right:
One of the buildings in the
Corning Glass Center complex.

THE SOUTHERN TIER

On the shores of Lake Chautauqua in New York's southwestern
corner is the Chautauqua Institute. It is an adult summer school
that offers more than two hundred courses stressing art, dance,
and music. At the nearby city of Jamestown are art galleries,
century-old houses, and a theater group.

In the city of Corning, visitors can tour the Corning Glass
Center, a unique museum that depicts the 3,500-year history of
glassmaking. Ithaca enjoys the sophistication of a college town
and proximity to natural wonders. Within a short drive of
downtown Ithaca are the bird sanctuary at Sapsucker Woods and
the stunning Taughannock Falls.

In the early 1980s, Elmira suffered the worst unemployment
rate of any city in the state. Then Japanese-owned firms bought

Hiking trails in Watkins Glen State Park give visitors spectacular views of magnificent gorges and waterfalls.

several of Elmira's vacant factory buildings, and workers there now produce subway cars and electronic components. Beloved writer Mark Twain spent many summers in Elmira and is buried in the city's Woodlawn Cemetery.

Daily automobile races are held from June to September at the famous Watkins Glen International-Montour Falls road racing course near Watkins Glen. Nearby Watkins Glen State Park is the southern tier's wilderness wonderland. Hiking trails there take visitors through magnificent gorges and past surging waterfalls.

The tri-city region of Binghamton, Endicott, and Johnson City features a center for the performing arts, a public observatory, and the Ross Park Zoo, which was established in the 1800s and is one of the nation's oldest zoos. To the east and south rise the forested Catskill Mountains. A drive through the Catskills leads to New York City—the world capital of excitement.

Chapter 10
A LOOK AT THE BIG APPLE

A LOOK AT THE BIG APPLE

"To tell the story of New York City would be to write a social history of the world," said British writer H.G. Wells. While it is true that no brief description can capture the scope and spirit of that amazing town, a borough-by-borough survey can bring out some of its flavor.

BROOKLYN

With almost 2.5 million people, Brooklyn is the largest of New York City's five boroughs. To its people, Brooklyn is far more than a subsidiary of the city. It is instead a great city in its own right.

Brooklyn's downtown area boasts busy shops and towering office buildings. Its neighborhoods range from the high-rise luxury of Brooklyn Heights to the burned-out and boarded-up buildings of Brownsville. Most Brooklyn neighborhoods have an ethnic character. In Bensonhurst, Italian families maintain close ties to their aging but beloved Catholic churches. Borough Park is the home of both Orthodox and Hasidic Jews. In Bedford-Stuyvesant, the city's largest black community, middle-class families have refurbished their turn-of-the-century row houses, and the buildings stand as a symbol of a neighborhood on the rise.

Brooklynites enjoy almost 6,000 acres (2,428 hectares) of parkland. In Prospect Park are the Brooklyn Museum, the Brooklyn Botanic Garden, and the landmark Soldiers and Sailors

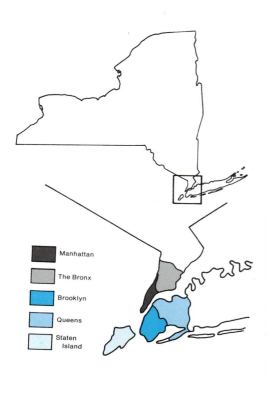

Brooklyn is home to such varied attractions as Coney Island (above) and a Botanic Garden (left).

Arch. Windows at the nearby New York Aquarium allow visitors to see beluga whales and a school of four-hundred-pound tiger sharks. After visiting the aquarium and the botanic garden, a traveler from England noted, "I consider that these two are among the great places in America."

At the southern tip of Brooklyn is Coney Island, one of New York City's most colorful landmarks. Generations of New Yorkers knew Coney Island as an amusement park famed for its dizzying rides. It is said that America's favorite snack food—the hot dog—originated on Coney Island pushcarts. The rides are gone now, but New Yorkers still come to Coney Island to walk its boardwalk and to swim off its windswept beaches.

QUEENS

Queens, the second most-populous borough, is a blend of old and new. Until World War II, much of Queens was open countryside. Then thousands of young families eager to build houses descended on it, and today Queens has miles of orderly suburbanlike single family houses. But Queens also has old neighborhoods whose residents have deep roots. Irish people in Woodside proudly claim that they, their parents, and their grandparents were all baptized at the same neighborhood Catholic church. The beautiful Forest Hills section, which was built up in the early 1900s, has the atmosphere and the architecture of a small town in old England. Neighborhood tradition is so strong in Queens that rarely does someone say, "I live in Queens." Instead, residents identify with a neighborhood, saying, "I live in Flushing," or "I live in Jamaica."

Corona Park in Queens was the site of New York World's Fairs in both 1939 and 1964. Remaining from the fairs are structures housing a science museum, an ice-skating rink, and a botancial garden. One of New York City's loveliest spots is Queens' Jamaica Bay Wildlife Refuge, where people hike on nature trails while wild geese honk above them—this within the borders of the nation's biggest and busiest city.

THE BRONX

The Bronx is a residential borough that houses New Yorkers of all social strata. At the borough's northern end stands the community of Riverdale, home to affluent lawyers and business owners. The South Bronx, only a short subway ride away, is one of America's most notorious slums.

Corona Park, in Queens, retains a few
reminders of two New York World's Fairs,
including the Unisphere (right).
Feeding time at the world-famous Bronx
Zoo (above) is a visitor's delight.

Despite the existence of slums, the Bronx boasts many
improving neighborhoods. The Grand Concourse, a marvelous
tree-lined boulevard, is being restored to its past glory. The Bronx
is the most Hispanic of all the boroughs, and Puerto Rican
community leaders are at the forefront of its rebirth movement.
Also aiding the community are Fordham University and Lehman
College, both of which have handsome campuses in the borough.

Bronx Park contains the world-famous Bronx Zoo, home to
more than 3,600 animals. The New York Botanical Gardens
features 250 acres (101 hectares) of herbs and flowers and a glass-
enclosed conservatory. The nearby Hall of Fame for Great
Americans is a circular colonnade containing the bronze busts of
ninety-five American heroes. Near the Harlem River stands
Yankee Stadium, home of the "Bronx Bombers" and a shrine that
has seen more baseball history than any other ballpark.

Staten Island commuters ride the famous Staten Island Ferry between their isolated borough and their jobs in the city.

STATEN ISLAND

Staten Island has the fewest people and is the most isolated of New York's five boroughs. Although linked to Brooklyn and New Jersey by bridges, Staten Island has no direct roadway to Manhattan. Manhattan commuters ride the famous Staten Island ferryboats. In 1988, a ride on the Staten Island Ferry cost only thirty-five cents, making it one of the greatest bargains in this otherwise very expensive city.

Staten Island communities resemble small towns rather than urban neighborhoods. Until the 1970s, the island was basically a rural farming area. Today, it is populated by homeowners who have suburban attitudes and refer to Manhattan as "the city."

Villages were established on Staten Island more than three hundred years ago, and the community has taken great pains to preserve and refurbish its historic buildings. The Conference House was a meeting place for American revolutionaries and British army officers on the eve of the American Revolution. The restored Voolezer House is believed to be the oldest elementary-school building in the United States.

A busy street corner in Harlem, one of the best known black communities in the world.

MANHATTAN

From the top of the Empire State Building, Manhattan looks like an army of glass-and-steel buildings. Indeed, three of the four tallest buildings in the world stand there, and very few single-family homes exist anywhere on the island. Viewed from above, the long rows of buildings form canyons through which flow rivers of toy-sized cars and people so small they resemble streams of ants. But Manhattan has an exciting human side that cannot be detected from the top of a building. Its human drama can be discovered by taking a long walk—a walk that begins in the north and ends on the island's southern tip.

The neighborhoods of Washington Heights and Inwood spread over north Manhattan. In Washington Heights is a museum called The Cloisters that specializes in art of the Middle Ages. To the south is Morningside Heights, site of Columbia University. Harlem, which lies to the east, is no longer the city's largest black community, but it remains the soul of black America. The very pulse of black literature, art, and music stems from that venerable community.

The vast expanse of Central Park, with its many cultural and recreational activities, is New York City's playground.

Central Park is an enormous island of greenery amid a labyrinth of concrete. The park contains a zoo, walkways, and countless statues. Facing Central Park are the American Museum of Natural History, where monstrous dinosaur bones stand; the futuristic Guggenheim Museum designed by architect Frank Lloyd Wright; and the world-famous Metropolitan Museum of Art. Some of the most expensive apartment buildings found anywhere on earth face Central Park. A tiny studio apartment costs more per month than the average teacher earns.

The Lincoln Center for the Performing Arts is the musical hub of the nation. Lincoln Center serves as headquarters for the New York Philharmonic Orchestra, the Metropolitan Opera, the New York City Ballet, and the Juilliard School of Music. South of Central Park is the cluster of buildings known as Rockefeller Center. Among the buildings is Radio City Music Hall, the world's largest indoor theater.

Broadway, which runs the length of Manhattan, is the Big Apple's busiest and zaniest avenue. At 42nd Street, Broadway

Soho, not far from Greenwich Village, has become New York's art center.

becomes Times Square, the heart of the theater district, and a place where all the contrasts of the big city come alive. On the sidewalks, it is common to see a street-corner preacher shouting a Gospel while standing outside an adult bookstore. Sin or salvation—they are both for sale in Times Square.

To the south lies Greenwich Village where, two generations ago, struggling artists lived because the rents were low. Today, rents in the ''Village'' are astronomical, but its cafes and bars remain meeting places for young novelists, painters, actors, and musicians. East of Broadway is the Lower East Side, a fabled neighborhood with a colorful history. It once housed immigrants from Eastern Europe, then impoverished Puerto Ricans moved in, and in the 1980s, artists and young professionals discovered the neighborhood.

The always busy streets of New York's Chinatown are lined with restaurants. Just next door is Little Italy, with its own concentration of eating places.

Anyone walking the length of Manhattan will certainly stop for lunch. The city offers restaurants ranging from stand-up pizzerias to elegant restaurants where the price of a dinner salad can be as high as ten dollars. Along Broadway south of Houston Street are Little Italy and Chinatown, two neighborhoods famed for their restaurants. Countless varieties of pasta dishes and other Italian delicacies are served in Little Italy. Chinatown centers on Mott Street, where many restaurants are housed in dingy basements, the customers sit at picnic tables, the waiters are grumpy—but the food tastes as if it has been made in heaven.

The crowded sidewalks of Manhattan ring with a dozen languages spoken by people of every race and ethnic origin.

Streets become narrow and winding as Broadway passes City Hall and enters the Financial District. Here the New York and American stock exchanges stand near the giant twin-towered World Trade Center. The southern half of the Financial District is the site of the original Dutch settlement and the city's oldest neighborhood. The yard surrounding Trinity Church dates back to 1681 and contains the grave of New Yorker Alexander Hamilton. Beyond Trinity Church, the waters of the Atlantic Ocean wash Manhattan's southern shores, marking the end of a walk through this amazing island.

The trek through Manhattan leads past shops displaying goods made in a thousand different lands. On the crowded sidewalks are the ring of a dozen languages and a flood of people representing every race and ethnic background. Manhattan is the heart and soul of New York—the world's most exciting city.

On Manhattan's southern tip nestles Battery Park. Across the waters from the park, the Statue of Liberty still welcomes those who are "yearning to breathe free." It is a fitting place to end the story of the Empire State. The last line of the Emma Lazarus poem inscribed on the statue's pedestal sums up what New York means to America: "I lift my lamp beside the golden door!"

FACTS AT A GLANCE

GENERAL INFORMATION

Statehood: July 26, 1788, eleventh state

Origin of Name: Named in honor of James Stuart, Duke of York and Albany (later King James II)

State Capital: Albany, since 1797

State Nickname: ''Empire State''; occasionally called ''Excelsior State''

State Flag: The state coat of arms is reproduced in the center of a dark blue field. The coat of arms consists of a mountain sunrise, a three-masted ship, and a Hudson River sloop all enclosed within a shield. Above the shield is an eagle on a globe; below is the state motto, *Excelsior*. On either side of the shield stand Liberty (with a discarded crown beneath one foot) and Justice.

State Motto: *Excelsior* (Ever upward)

State Bird: Bluebird

State Animal: Beaver

State Fish: Trout

State Flower: Rose

State Tree: Sugar maple

State Fruit: Apple

State Gem: Garnet

State Song: None

POPULATION

Population: 17,990,455, second among the states (1990 census)

Population Density: 366 people per sq. mi. (141 people per km²)

Population Distribution: 85 percent of the people live in cities or towns. Just over 50 percent of New York State residents live in the New York City metropolitan area, the twelfth-largest metropolitan area in the world. New York City itself is the largest city in the state, the largest city in the nation, and the ninth-largest city in the world.

New York	7,322,564
Buffalo	328,123
Rochester	231,636
Yonkers	188,082
Syracuse	163,860
Albany	101,082
Utica	68,637
New Rochelle	67,265
Mount Vernon	67,153

(Population figures according to the 1990 census)

Population Growth: New York's population increased by more than four times in the decades from the 1780 census to the 1820 census. Most newcomers came from the New England states to clear new lands for farms or to open shops in the growing urban areas. In the 1840s and 1850s, northern Europeans arrived from England, Ireland, and Germany in such numbers that by 1855 a quarter of the state's population was European-born. After 1890, a wave of southern and eastern Europeans came from Italy and Greece, along with Jews and Poles from Russia. Immigration from Europe slowed in the first half of the twentieth century due to the disruptions of World Wars I and II and the Great Depression. After 1950, the largest numbers of newcomers were from Puerto Rico and from the southern states. By 1960, New York was the most-populous state in the Union. But by the 1970 census, California had become the top state in population.

Year	Population
1790	340,120
1820	1,372,812
1840	2,428,921
1860	3,880,735
1880	5,082,871
1900	7,268,894
1920	10,385,227
1940	13,479,142
1960	16,782,304
1970	18,241,266
1980	17,558,072
1990	17,990,455

The Niagara River, which forms part of the boundary between New York and Canada, plunges into a steep gorge to form the natural wonder that is Niagara Falls.

GEOGRAPHY

Borders: Lake Ontario and the Canadian provinces of Ontario and Quebec border New York on the north. Lakes Erie and Ontario and the Canadian province of Ontario form the western border. Vermont, Massachusetts, and Connecticut form New York's eastern border, with the Atlantic Ocean on the southeast. New Jersey and Pennsylvania are to the south.

Highest Point: Mount Marcy in the Adirondacks, 5,344 ft. (1,629 m) above sea level

Lowest Point: Sea level, at the Atlantic Ocean

Greatest Distances: North to south—307 mi. **(494 km)**
East to west—314 mi.(⁻ 5 ˎ m)

Area: 49,108 sq. mi. (127,189 km²)

Rank in Area Among the States: Thirtieth

Rivers: New York's principal river is the Hudson, which originates in the Adirondack Mountains, winds southward through eastern New York, and empties into New York Bay. In its southern course, the Hudson has cut a deep gorge, creating the beautiful rock cliffs called the Palisades. The Mohawk, principal tributary of the Hudson, originates in central New York, flows east and south, and enters the Hudson at Cohoes. Rivers that create the international boundary between New York and Canada are the St. Lawrence in the north and the Niagara in the northwest. The Delaware River forms part of the border between New York and Pennsylvania. Other important rivers in New York include the Genesee; the Oswego and its branch, the Seneca; the Susquehanna; and the Allegheny. The East River is an important New York City waterway, separating Manhattan and Long Island.

Oxbow lakes such as this one in the Adirondacks are formed when a river changes course and leaves behind an arc of water that becomes cut off from the main river.

New York's major waterfalls include massive Niagara Falls, 1,060 ft. (323 m) wide with a drop of 167 ft. (51m) on the United States side, and 3,010 ft. (917 m) wide with a drop of 158 ft. (48 m) on the Canadian side. The 215-ft. (66-m) Taughannock Falls near Cayuga Lake is among the longest falls east of the Rocky Mountains.

Lakes: New York boasts more than eight thousand lakes. Lake Oneida and Lake George are the two largest lakes wholly within the state. Lake Champlain lies on the border between New York and Vermont and extends into Canada. Lakes Erie and Ontario form part of the international boundary with Canada. The Finger Lakes lie in central New York; Seneca and Cayuga are the largest of the Finger Lakes. Saranac Lake and Lake Placid in the Adirondacks, and Chautauqua Lake in the southwest, are popular vacation and resort areas. The New York shoreline includes 371 mi. (597 km) along Lakes Erie and Ontario, 174 mi. (280 km) along Lake Champlain, and 192 mi. (309 km) along the St. Lawrence and Niagara rivers. New York's coastline along the Atlantic Ocean measures 1,850 mi. (2,977 km), tracing its bays and inlets, or 127 mi. (204 km) of general coastline if stretched along an imaginary straight line. New York City has one of the world's greatest natural harbors. Buffalo is the state's major lake port, accessible to oceangoing ships by way of the St. Lawrence Seaway.

Topography: Geographers divide New York into seven major regions: the St. Lawrence Lowland, the Adirondack Upland, and the Great Lakes Lowland (sometimes called the Erie-Ontario Lowland) in the north; and the Hudson-Mohawk Lowland, the New England Upland, the Atlantic Coastal Plain, and the Appalachian Plateau in the south.

The St. Lawrence Lowland, in the north, stretches along the south bank of the St. Lawrence River from Thousand Islands at Alexandria Bay to the Canadian border. The lowlands are only 18 to 20 mi. (29 to 32 km) wide, with an average elevation of 300 ft. (91 m) above sea level. The Adirondack Upland, in northeastern New York, lies south of the St. Lawrence Lowland and contains the Adirondack Mountains, part of the great Canadian Shield. In New York, the Adirondacks range in height from 2,000 ft. (610 m) to 5,344 ft. (1,629 m) at Mt. Marcy. Clear lakes, swift streams, and many waterfalls can be found throughout the region. In northwestern New York, the Great Lakes Lowland borders Lakes Erie and Ontario, extending 5 to 40 mi. (8 to 64 km) inland from the lakeshores. Most of the region is low-lying and swampy, but there are hilly areas resulting from glacial deposits. In the west, an east-west limestone ridge has created the best-known waterfall in North America, Niagara Falls.

In central and southeastern New York, the Hudson-Mohawk Lowland follows the river valleys of the Hudson and Mohawk. The New England Upland occupies the southern half of New York's eastern border. It extends from Lake Champlain south to Manhattan Island and includes the Taconic Range (known locally as the Berkshires), the southern part of the Hudson River Valley, and part of New York City. The Atlantic Coastal Plain, at the southeastern tip of the state, includes Staten Island and Long Island as well as the coastal area.

The Appalachian (or Allegheny) Plateau is the state's largest land area. Lying south of the Great Lakes Lowland and west of the Hudson-Mohawk Lowland, it occupies most of southern New York and includes the Catskill Mountains in the east and the Finger Lakes region in the center.

Climate: New York's climate varies widely across the state, depending on elevation and proximity to large bodies of water such as the Atlantic Ocean or Lakes Ontario and Erie. Generally, summers are warm and winters are cold. New York City's average August temperature is 73° F. (23° C) contrasted to an August average of 62° F. (17° C) in the Adirondacks. In February, temperatures average 33° F. (0.6° C) in New York City, and 14° F. (-10° C) in the Adirondacks. The state's highest recorded temperature was 108° F. (42° C) at Troy on July 22, 1926; its lowest recorded temperature was -52° F. (-47° C) at Stillwater Reservoir in the Adirondacks on February 18, 1979. General precipitation averages 32 to 54 in. (81 to 137 cm) across the state. Snowfall averages 26 in. (66 cm) each year in New York City and along the coast, but reaches 122 in. (310 cm) in the Adirondacks. Rochester and Buffalo are in the "snowbelt" area around the Great Lakes, and Syracuse gets more snow than any other city in the nation, an average of 108 in. (274 cm) each year.

NATURE

Trees: New York has some 150 tree species, including ash, beech, birch, red cedar, cherry, fir, hemlock, laurel, maple, oak, shortleaf and white pines, spruce, sweet gum, and tulip trees.

Wild Plants: Apples, berried shrubs, buttercups, clover, white daisies and black-eyed Susans, goldenrod, goldthreads, grapes, mosses and lichens, devil's paintbrush, peaches, Indian pipes, plums, Queen Anne's lace, wild roses, starflowers, strawberries, trilliums, violets

Animals: Beaver, deer, fox, mink, muskrat, opossum, otter, porcupine, rabbit, raccoon, skunk, woodchuck

Birds: More than 260 species of birds spend some part of the year in New York State, including bluebirds, catbirds, crows, ducks, grouse, hawks, meadowlarks, orioles, owls, partridges, pheasants, plovers, robins, snipes, sparrows, swallows, chimney swifts, thrushes, woodcocks, woodpeckers, and wrens.

Fish: Among New York's four hundred or so species of freshwater fish are bass, crappie, perch, pickerel, pike, sunfish, and trout. Ocean and saltwater fish include bass, bluefish, flounder, pollack, shad, shellfish, swordfish, tuna, and weakfish.

GOVERNMENT

The government of New York, like the federal government, is divided into three branches—legislative, executive, and judicial. The legislative branch is made up of a senate with 61 members, and an assembly with 150 members. Members of both houses are elected to two-year terms. The legislature votes on new laws and determines how state revenues will be spent.

The executive branch, headed by the governor, administers the law. The governor is elected to a four-year term and may be reelected an unlimited number of times. The state constitution gives the governor power to veto legislation, grant pardons, and serve as commander-in-chief of the state militia. The governor has the power to appoint most department heads.

The judicial branch interprets laws and tries cases. The state's highest court, the court of appeals, is made up of a chief justice and six associate justices, who are elected to fourteen-year terms. The second-highest court in New York is the appellate court, which hears appeals from the lower courts. Appellate-court justices are appointed by the governor. The lowest court, where most cases are heard, is called the supreme court. Supreme-court justices are elected by the voters to fourteen-year terms.

Number of Counties: 62

U.S. Representatives: 34

Electoral Votes: 36

Voting Qualifications: Citizen of the United States, at least eighteen years of age, with ninety days residency in New York and ninety days residency in the county

EDUCATION

A sixteen-member board of regents supervises education in New York. Members of the board of regents are elected to seven-year terms by the legislature. They receive no compensation. The regents appoint a commissioner of education, who heads a department of education. The department of education oversees some 750 school districts. More than 2.5 million students are enrolled in New York elementary and secondary day schools. About 17 percent of all elementary and secondary students are enrolled in private schools. School attendance is required of children between the ages of six and sixteen.

The State University of New York (SUNY), created by the legislature in 1948, is one of the nation's largest university systems. Among its more than seventy units are the state universities at Albany, Binghamton, Buffalo, and Stony Brook. Some sixteen SUNY colleges are located throughout the state. Additional SUNY colleges specialize in health, science, and technology. New York has about 220 private colleges and universities, including Columbia University, Barnard College, Fordham University, Jewish Theological Seminary of America, Juilliard School of Music, Manhattan College, New York University, Pratt Institute, St. John's University, Sarah Lawrence College, and the Union Theological Institute, all in New York City; Bard College, in Annondale-on-Hudson; Colgate University, in Hamilton; Cornell University, in Ithaca; Rensselaer Polytechnic Institute, in Troy; Rochester University, in Rochester; Skidmore College, in Saratoga Springs; Syracuse University, in Syracuse; and Vassar College, in Poughkeepsie. In addition, the United States Military Academy is located at West Point, and the United States Coast Guard Academy is at Kings Point.

ECONOMY AND INDUSTRY

Principal Products

Agriculture: Apples, beans, beets, cabbage, carrots, cauliflower, celery, cherries, clover, corn, dairy products, eggs, greenhouse and nursery products, hay, honey, maple syrup, potatoes, poultry, veal and other meat products, wine grapes, beef cattle, hogs, lambs, sheep, ducks

Manufacturing: Aircraft, cameras and photographic equipment, chemicals, computers, copy machines, drugs, electrical and nonelectrical machinery, food products, furniture, glass, paper, periodicals, printing equipment, radio and television equipment, steel, textiles and wearing apparel, toys, transportation equipment, wine

Natural Resources: Commercial fish and shellfish, emery, garnets, granite, gravel, gypsum, lead, limestone, lumber, oil and natural gas, salt, sand, talc, zinc

Business and Trade: Among the fifty states, New York ranks first in wholesale trade and second only to California in retail trade, manufacturing, and the total number of production workers employed.

Four of the five largest banks in the nation are located in New York City: Citibank, the nation's largest; Chase Manhattan Bank; Manufacturers Hanover Trust Co.; Morgan Guaranty Trust Co.; and Chemical Bank. In all, the assets of New York banks are about one fifth of the total assets of all of the banks in the United States. In addition, more than a hundred foreign banks are located in New York City.

Manhattan's Wall Street, home of the New York Stock Exchange, the American Stock Exchange, and hundreds of brokerage firms, has long been the financial center of the United States, and even the world.

Many of the nation's largest corporations have their headquarters in or around New York City, including American Telephone and Telegraph (AT&T), Colgate-Palmolive, International Business Machines (IBM), Mobil Oil, Pan Am Corp., Texaco, RCA, and Woolworth. Eastman Kodak has its headquarters in Rochester.

Communication: New York leads the nation in the production of books, magazines, and newspapers. New York has 90 daily newspapers and 750 weeklies. Two newspapers, the *New York Times* and the *Wall Street Journal*, are circulated nationally. Other large-circulation newspapers published in New York are the *New York Daily News*, the *New York Post*, *Newsday* (on Long Island), the *Buffalo News*, the *Binghamton Press & Sun Bulletin*, the *Rochester Democrat-Chronicle*, and the *Syracuse Post Standard*.

New York has more than three hundred AM and FM radio stations and about forty television stations. All three major television networks—NBC, ABC, and CBS—make their headquarters in New York City.

Transportation: New York has nearly 110,000 mi. (177,000 km) of roads and highways. Fourteen thousand mi. (22,530 km) of these are state highways and parkways. The 4,260-ft. (1,298-m) Verrazano-Narrows Bridge, which connects Brooklyn and Staten Island, is one of the world's longest suspension bridges. Other noted bridges include the Brooklyn Bridge, connecting Brooklyn and Manhattan; the George Washington Bridge, which spans the Hudson from New York City to New Jersey; and the Peace Bridge, linking Buffalo and Fort Erie in Canada.

The New York State Barge Canal System—which includes the Champlain, Oswego, Cayuga, Seneca, and Erie canals, covers 800 mi. (1,287 km), and contains fifty-seven locks—is an important part of the state's transportation system.

New York City is one of the world's largest and busiest seaports. Other important ports are at Albany, Buffalo, Ogdensburg, Oswego, and Rochester.

New York has nearly five hundred public and private airports. The John F. Kennedy International Airport in New York City is the nation's busiest international airport. New York City is also served by LaGuardia Airport and Newark (New Jersey) International Airport. In addition, Long Island/MacArthur Airport, Westchester County Airport, and Teterboro (New Jersey) Airport all serve as alternatives to the major airports. New York is served by about thirty railroads, which operate on about 4,000 mi. (6,437 km) of track. New York City is the major stop on the Boston-Washington high-speed Amtrak line. The New York City subway system is the world's largest.

SOCIAL AND CULTURAL LIFE

Museums: The Metropolitan Museum of Art, facing New York City's Central Park, is one of the world's major museums. Its huge collection includes Greek, Roman, Medieval, European, African, Pacific Islands, Far Eastern, Near Eastern, and twentieth-century works of art. The Museum of Modern Art was one of the first museums dedicated only to modern art. More than a million visitors a year come to see the works of Picasso, Chagall, Kandinsky, Mondrian, Matisse, Monet, Rousseau, Van Gogh, Renoir, and others. Among the more than 150 other museums in New York City are the Guggenheim Museum, which is housed in a building designed by Frank Lloyd Wright; the Cloisters Museum of Medieval Religious Art and Architecture; the American Museum of Natural History; the Museum of the American Indian; the Whitney Museum; the Brooklyn Museum; and the Brooklyn Children's Museum.

Museums outside of New York City include the Buffalo Museum of Science and the Albright Art Gallery, in Buffalo; the Utica Children's Museum, in Utica; the Emerson Museum of Art, in Syracuse; the Shaker Museum, in Old Chatham; the Albany Institute of History and Art and the New York State Museum, in Albany.

Specialized museums include the Corning Museum of Glass, in Corning; the Erie Canal Museum, in Syracuse; the Farmers' Museum, in Cooperstown; and the Gladding International Sport Fishing Museum in South Otselic. In addition, New York is home to the Boxing Hall of Fame, in Canastota; the Speed Skating Hall of Fame, in Newburg; the Trotting Horse Hall of Fame, in Goshen; the National Soccer Hall of Fame, in Oneonta; the National Motor Racing Hall of Fame, in Watkins Glen; and most famous of all, the Baseball Hall of Fame, in Cooperstown.

Libraries: The New York State Library, in Albany, has a general collection of about 4.5 million items. The New York Public Library has more than 7 million volumes and is one of the nation's best research libraries. In addition, New York City is served by three independent library systems with more than two hundred branches and combined holdings of nearly 12 million volumes. The Buffalo Public Library has the excellent Grosvenor Collection. Rochester, Syracuse, and Yonkers also have large public library systems. Large college and university libraries in New York include those of Columbia University, in New York City; Cornell University, in Ithaca; the State University of New York, in Buffalo; and Syracuse University. The University of Rochester has one of America's largest music collections. The Pierpont Morgan Library in New York City is the most renowned private library.

Performing Arts: New York City's Lincoln Center for the Performing Arts is the nation's largest such complex. Lincoln Center also houses the Juilliard School of Music. Avery Fisher Hall is home to the New York Philharmonic Orchestra. Carnegie Hall, long the home of the Philharmonic, has been restored and is used by many visiting American and European orchestras and artists. Alice Tulley Hall is used for chamber music and recitals. The famed Metropolitan Opera performs at the Metropolitan Opera House. The New York State Theater is home to both the New York City Ballet and the New York City Opera. Buffalo, Brooklyn, Long Island, Syracuse, Rochester, and Albany also have symphony orchestras. The Syracuse Opera and the Lake George Opera Festival at Glens Falls are noted opera companies.

New York City's theater district has the nation's largest concentration of theaters. There are about a thousand premieres in New York theaters every year. In the summer, many plays, musicals, and concerts are presented in the parks.

Sports and Recreation: New York has nine professional sports teams. Included are the New York Yankees of the American League and the New York Mets of the

National League, in professional baseball; the Buffalo Bills, the New York Giants, and the New York Jets of the National Football League; the Buffalo Sabres, the New York Islanders, and the New York Rangers of the National Hockey League; and the New York Knicks of the National Basketball Association. The annual New York Marathon attracts thousands of runners, including many of the best from overseas. The Belmont Stakes, at Elmont, is part of the "triple crown" of horse racing, which includes the Kentucky Derby and the Preakness Stakes. In tennis, the U.S. Open is held each year in Flushing Meadows.

At the Bronx Zoo, more than three hundred species of birds and animals are housed in surroundings similar to their native habitats. The Brooklyn Botanic Garden has more than twelve thousand species of plants, including nine hundred kinds of roses. The New York Botanical Garden, in addition to its plant and flower displays, has extensive scholarly and public services including a library, herbarium, and school of horticulture. Nearly twenty thousand marine animals, ranging from two-ton beluga whales to tiny tropical fish, can be seen at the New York Aquarium. Marine Park in Brooklyn is a sprawling seaside wilderness area and wildlife refuge on the very edge of America's largest city.

With about 150 state parks and 60 forest areas, New York affords ample opportunity for everyone to engage in outdoor activities. New York's eight thousand lakes and 70,000 mi. (112,654 km) of rivers and streams yield such popular sports fish as walleye, bass, crappie, trout, salmon, muskie, and pike. Visitors can enjoy hiking, camping, canoeing, whitewater rafting, horseback riding, golf, sailing, swimming, backpacking, and cycling. In the winter, there is downhill and cross-country skiing, skating, ice fishing, and photography.

Historic Sites And Landmarks:

Battle of Saratoga National Historic Park is near Stillwater. The surrender of General Burgoyne at this spot on October 17, 1777 marked a major turning point in the American Revolution.

Castle Clinton National Monument in New York City was built prior to the War of 1812 and served for many years as a depot for immigrants. It has been completely restored and reopened as a national monument.

Eleanor Roosevelt National Historic Site at Hyde Park was Mrs. Roosevelt's country home (called Val-kill) from 1925 until her death in 1962.

Federal Hall National Memorial in New York City is the site of the first United States capitol (1785-1790), and here George Washington was inaugurated as first president of the United States in 1789.

Fort Ticonderoga at Ticonderoga was captured from the British by Ethan Allen on May 10, 1775, and was later recaptured and held by the British until the surrender of General Burgoyne at Saratoga in 1777.

Franklin D. Roosevelt National Historic Site at Hyde Park is the burial place of the thirty-second president of the United States. Its Roosevelt Library and Museum contain many of the president's papers, books, and other personal belongings.

Millions of people traveled to New York when the United States celebrated the centennial of the Statue of Liberty on July 4, 1986. One of the highlights of the huge weekend birthday party was a spectacular fireworks display.

General Grant National Memorial in New York City is a monument that marks the burial place of Ulysses S. Grant, eighteenth president of the United States and victorious Civil War general.

John Brown State Historic Site in East Elba is the homestead and burial place of abolitionist John Brown, who was executed for leading a raid on the U.S. Arsenal at Harpers Ferry, Virginia, in 1859.

Martin Van Buren National Historic Site at Kinderhook is the thirty-six-room mansion where Martin Van Buren, eighth president of the United States, lived from 1841 until his death in 1862.

Millard Fillmore House National Landmark in Aurora was the home of the thirteenth president of the United States from 1825 to 1830.

Oriskany Battlefield State Historic Site at Oriskany is the site of the decisive battle in 1777 that helped lead to the British abandonment of nearby Fort Stanwix. Here, a group of patriots under the leadership of General Nicholas Herkimer defeated a combined British, Tory, and Iroquois force. The battle is reenacted every year on August 6.

Schuyler Mansion State Historic Site in Albany is the eighteenth-century Georgian mansion of General Philip Schuyler, father-in-law of Alexander Hamilton and Federalist politician in the early years of the republic. It is noted for its architectural excellence and outstanding collection of colonial and Federal-period furnishings.

Statue of Liberty National Monument on Liberty Island, New York City, was a gift from the people of France. The statue has stood on Liberty Island (formerly Bedloe's Island) since 1886 as a symbol of freedom and American ideals. It was renovated, in part with contributions from American schoolchildren, and reopened to the public on July 4, 1986.

Theodore Roosevelt National Inaugural Site is in Buffalo. Following the assassination of President William McKinley in 1901, Theodore Roosevelt was sworn in as the twenty-sixth president of the United States in the library of a Buffalo lawyer named Ansley Wilcox. The Wilcox House has now been restored and preserved as a national monument.

Women's Rights National Historic Park in Seneca Falls is the site of the first Women's Rights Convention (1848) called by Elizabeth Cady Stanton. More than three hundred people met to discuss the social condition of women. A Declaration of Sentiments, advocating the right of women to vote, was signed by sixty-eight women and thirty-two men.

Vanderbilt Mansion National Historic Site at Hyde Park, an opulent fifty-room mansion built between 1896 and 1898 by Frederick W. Vanderbilt, grandson of Cornelius Vanderbilt, has been a national historic site since 1940.

Other Interesting Places to Visit:

Baseball Hall of Fame is in Cooperstown. From Hank Aaron to Cy Young, the greatest baseball players of all time are enshrined in this combined Hall of Fame and baseball museum.

Brooklyn Bridge in New York City, one of the great wonders of the world when it was built in 1883, is still a major New York landmark.

Central Park in New York City is an extended area of grass, gardens, walkways, ponds, bridges, malls, playgrounds, a theater, a restaurant, and a small zoo, covering 840 acres (97 hectares) in the heart of Manhattan.

Empire State Building in New York City has been a world landmark since its completion in 1931. Although no longer the world's tallest building, it is still one of the most famous.

Empire State Plaza and State Capitol in Albany is a complex that includes the state capitol, a convention center, a performing-arts center, the state museum, a cultural center, government office buildings, and the New York State Vietnam Memorial.

Niagara Falls in Niagara Falls comprises the 182-ft. (55-m) American Falls, in New York, and the adjacent 173-ft. (53-m) Horseshoe Falls in Ontario, Canada. Together they form one of the great natural wonders of North America.

Rockefeller Center in New York City is a complex of twenty-one high-rise office buildings that includes thirty restaurants, a museum of mural paintings, several television studios, convention halls, and Radio City Music Hall.

Staten Island Ferry, between New York City and Staten Island, offers a magnificent view of the Manhattan skyline and the Statue of Liberty.

Times Square in New York City is the heart of the theater district, with more than thirty-five nearby theaters.

United Nations Headquarters in New York City includes the thirty-nine-story glass and marble tower of the Secretariat Building. Other buildings are the General Assembly Building, the Conference Building, and the Dag Hammarskjold Library.

Wall Street Financial District in New York City contains the world's largest concentration of banks, brokerage firms, and financial houses. Included are the New York Stock Exchange and the American Stock Exchange.

United States Military Academy at West Point is the nation's foremost training school for army officers; it also has the world's largest military museum.

World Trade Center in New York City comprises twin towers that are New York's tallest buildings. The observation deck in the north tower affords a spectacular view; New York's highest restaurant is in the other tower.

IMPORTANT DATES

A.D. 700—Mound Builders in Mississippi and Ohio river valleys extend their influence eastward into New York

1524—Giovanni Da Verrazano of Italy becomes the first European to enter New York's harbor

c. 1570—The Iroquois Federation is established

1609—Henry Hudson sails up the Hudson River as far as Albany under the Dutch flag; Samuel de Champlain marches into New York from Canada under the French flag

1624—Dutch West India Company settles eighteen families at present-day Albany

1626—Peter Minuit buys Manhattan Island from the Manhattan Indians, reportedly paying in trinkets worth some $24

1664—British take over Dutch New Netherland and rename it New York

1725—First newspaper in the region, the *New York Gazette*, published in New York City

1734—Trial of John Peter Zenger, printer, establishes the principle of freedom of the press

1775—Ethan Allen and Benedict Arnold capture British Fort Ticonderoga

1776 — British capture New York City; Mother Ann Lee establishes the first United States Shaker community at Watervliet

1777 — Battle of Saratoga marks a turning point in the American Revolution

1779 — General Washington sends troops against Britain's ally, the Iroquois; destruction of villages, fields, and livestock breaks the Iroquois' hold on the territory forever

1784 — State legislature establishes an agency to direct state education system

1785 — New York City becomes national capital for four years

1788 — New York enters the Union as the eleventh state, July 26

1789 — George Washington is inaugurated first president of the United States in New York City

1802 — United States Military Academy at West Point opens

1807 — Robert Fulton's steamship, the *Clermont*, steams from New York City to Albany in thirty-two hours

1818 — New York State Library founded in Albany

1825 — Erie Canal completed, running from Albany to Buffalo

1827 — Slavery abolished in New York

1830 — Joseph Smith founds the Mormon Church (Church of Latter-Day Saints) and publishes *The Book of Mormon* at Fayette

1831 — New York's first railroad, the Mohawk & Hudson, opens, running from Albany to Schenectady

1836 — Martin Van Buren elected eighth president of the United States; New York State Museum, the nation's first state museum, founded in Albany

1839 — Antirent Wars begin in Columbia and Delaware counties

1848 — Seneca Falls Convention proclaims women's rights

1850 — Millard Fillmore takes office as thirteenth president of the United States

1854 — First Young Men's Christian Association (YMCA) meets at Buffalo

1863 — Antidraft riots rock New York City

1874 — First Chautauqua Assembly meets at Lake Chautauqua

1881—Chester A. Arthur takes office as twenty-first president of the United States

1883—Brooklyn Bridge completed, the world's longest at the time

1884—Grover Cleveland is elected twenty-second president of the United States

1886—Statue of Liberty unveiled in New York harbor

1892—Grover Cleveland elected twenty-fourth president of the United States; immigration-processing center built at Ellis Island

1894—Present state constitution adopted, to be amended nearly two hundred times in the next century

1898—Greater New York formed by uniting the five boroughs of Brooklyn, Queens, the Bronx, Staten Island, and Manhattan

1901—President William McKinley is assassinated at Pan-American Exposition in Buffalo; Theodore Roosevelt takes office as twenty-sixth president of the United States

1911—Fire strikes New York City's Triangle Shirtwaist factory, killing 146 workers

1918—The New York State Barge Canal is completed; it links Lake Champlain and the Hudson River to Lakes Erie and Ontario

1926—Nation's first coast-to-coast radio network, the National Broadcasting Company (NBC), established in New York City

1928—General Electric experimental television station W2XAD (now WRGB) in Schenectady broadcasts the first dramatic production on television

1929—Stock-market crash on Wall Street sets the stage for the worldwide Great Depression

1931—Empire State Building in New York City, the world's tallest building for many decades, is completed

1932—Franklin Delano Roosevelt is elected thirty-second president of the United States; Winter Olympic Games held at Lake Placid

1939—New York hosts a World's Fair at Flushing Meadows; Baseball Hall of Fame opens in Cooperstown

1941—Nation's first commercial television station, WNBT, begins broadcasting in New York City

1947—Jackie Robinson signs with the Brooklyn Dodgers, first black professional baseball player in the major leagues; he also wins title "Rookie of the Year"

1948 — The State University of New York is established

1952 — United Nations headquarters building is completed in New York City

1959 — St. Lawrence Seaway opens, admitting oceangoing ships from New York harbor to Great Lakes ports

1961 — Giant hydroelectric power plant at Niagara Falls begins operation

1964 — Harlem race riots in New York City; New York hosts a World's Fair at Flushing Meadows; Verrazano-Narrows Bridge opens in New York City

1965 — New York City blacked out by major electrical power failure

1971 — Riot at Attica Prison kills forty-three persons

1975 — New York State faces a financial crisis

1977 — Second major New York City blackout

1978 — Community evacuated due to toxic chemical pollution of Love Canal

1980 — Winter Olympic Games held at Lake Placid

1984 — Congresswoman Geraldine Ferraro of Queens is nominated Democratic party's candidate for vice-president of United States

1986 — Renovation and centennial party for the Statue of Liberty

1987 — Near-crash panics New York Stock Exchange with worldwide repercussions

1989 — New York City elects its first black mayor, David N. Dinkins

1990 — The largest ticker-tape parade in New York City history is held for African National Congress leader Nelson Mandela

WOODY ALLEN

IMPORTANT PEOPLE

Bella Savitzky Abzug (1920-   ), born in New York City; congresswoman and leading figure in the women's liberation movement; U.S. representative (1971-77)

Woody Allen (1935-   ), born Allen Stewart Konigsberg in New York City; actor, director, writer, comedian; won two Academy Awards for writing and directing the film *Annie Hall* (1977)

Chester Alan Arthur (1829-1886), twenty-first president of the United States (1881-85); collector of Port of New York (1871-79); vice-president of United States (1881); became president when James A. Garfield was assassinated

John Jacob Astor (1763-1848), fur trader and millionaire founder of a dynasty of New York society figures who invested in Manhattan Island real estate; left an estate estimated at $20 million

George Balanchine (1904-1983), born George Melitonovitch Balanchinvadze in Russia; choreographer; made his home in New York City where he founded the School of American Ballet (1933) and the New York City Ballet (1948)

James Arthur Baldwin (1924-1987), born in New York City; writer and forceful critic of racial discrimination in the United States; his novel *Go Tell It on the Mountain* (1953) was set in Harlem

Leonard Bernstein (1919-1990), conductor, composer, pianist, and musical director of the New York Philharmonic Orchestra (1958-69); best known for musicals *On the Town* (1944), *Wonderful Town* (1953), and *West Side Story* (1957)

Mathew B. Brady (1822?-1896), born in Warren County; pioneer photographer who documented the Civil War on film

William Cullen Bryant (1794-1878), poet and journalist; editor (1829) of New York City's *Evening Post*; strongly supported free speech and organized labor and strongly opposed slavery; helped establish Central Park and the Metropolitan Museum of Art

William Frank Buckley, Jr. (1925-   ), born in New York City; advocate of political conservatism; host of a national television talk show; founder and editor of the magazine *National Review*

Saint Frances Xavier Cabrini (1850-1917), first U.S. citizen to be declared a saint by the Roman Catholic Church (1946); founded New York City's Columbus Hospital (1892); named patron saint of emigrants (1950)

Shirley Anita St. Hill Chisholm (1924-   ), born in Brooklyn; political leader; state legislator (1964-68); first black woman to be a U.S. representative (1969-83), and the first to mount a serious campaign for the Democratic party's nomination for the United States presidency (1972)

Mark Wayne Clark (1896-1984), born in Madison Barracks; career army officer; U.S. general in World War II; U.N. commander in Korea; U.S. commander during the Korean War (1950-53)

(Stephen) Grover Cleveland (1837-1908), twenty-second (1885-89) and twenty-fourth (1893-97) president of the United States; mayor of Buffalo (1881); governor (1882)

De Witt Clinton (1769-1828), born in Little Britain; public official; state legislator (1797 and 1802); U.S. senator (1802-03); mayor of New York City (1803-15); governor (1817-28); vigorously and successfully pushed for the building of the Erie Canal

CHESTER A. ARTHUR

SHIRLEY CHISHOLM

GROVER CLEVELAND

DE WITT CLINTON

GEORGE CLINTON

THOMAS E. DEWEY

JOE DiMAGGIO

GEORGE EASTMAN

George Clinton (1739-1812), born in Little Britain; soldier and public official; governor (1777-95); vice-president of the United States (1805-12)

Thomas Cole (1801-1848), English-born painter who moved to the U.S.; created the Hudson River School of painting

James Fenimore Cooper (1789-1851), author and social critic; used American history, backgrounds, and characters in his novels, two of which—*The Pioneers* (1823) and *The Deerslayer* (1841)—were set near his boyhood home of Cooperstown

Aaron Copland (1900-1990), born in New York City; composer; his music often incorporated such elements as folk themes and jazz; awarded the 1945 Pulitzer Prize in music for *Appalachian Spring,* the 1948 Academy Award for music in the film *The Heiress,* and the 1964 United States Presidential Medal of Freedom

Mario Matthew Cuomo (1932-   ), born in New York City; political leader; first Italian-American elected governor of New York (1982); his rousing keynote speech before the Democratic party convention in 1984 won national attention

Thomas Edmund Dewey (1902-1971), lawyer and public official; hard hitting special prosecutor of New York rackets and vice; governor (1943-55); twice the Republican party nominee for the United States presidency; his second defeat (in 1948 to Harry Truman) was a stunning upset that ended his political career

Joseph Paul (Joe) DiMaggio (1914-   ), professional baseball player; New York Yankees outfielder (1936-51); named the American League's Most Valuable Player in 1939, 1941, and 1947; elected to the National Baseball Hall of Fame in 1955

George Eastman (1854-1932), born in Waterville; inventor and manufacturer; developed flexible roll films (1884) and a lightweight camera, the Kodak (1888)

Geraldine Anne Ferraro (1935-   ), born in Newburgh; lawyer, politician; U.S. representative (1978-84); first woman nominated by a major political party (Democratic party) as its candidate for vice-president (1984)

Millard Fillmore (1800-1874), born in Locke; thirteenth president of the United States (1850-53); U.S. representative (1833-35, 1837-43); vice-president of United States (1849-50)

James Vincent Forrestal (1892-1949), born in Beacon; naval aviator and financier; secretary of the navy (1944-47); as first U.S. secretary of defense (1947-49), he helped build up the nation's fleet into the largest in the world

Henry Louis (Lou) Gehrig (1903-1941), born in New York City; professional baseball player; New York Yankees first baseman (1924-39); retired from baseball with a rare nerve disease (amyotrophic lateral sclerosis), still often called Lou Gehrig's disease; elected to the National Baseball Hall of Fame in 1939

George Gershwin (1898-1937), born in Brooklyn; composer; received the first Pulitzer Prize ever awarded for a musical comedy with *Of Thee I Sing* (1931); also noted for the symphonic works *Rhapsody in Blue* (1924) and *An American in Paris* (1928), and the popular folk opera *Porgy and Bess* (1935)

Jay Gould (1836-1892), born near Roxbury; financier and railroad owner; precipitated the 1869 "Black Friday" panic when he tried to monopolize the New York City gold market; manipulated stock to take control of the Erie Railroad and become its president (1868)

Asa Gray (1810-1888), born in Sauquoit; botanist whose *Manual of Botany* influenced classification and interpretation of North American plant life for over a century; taught at Harvard (1842-73), initiating the university's present-day world famous herbarium

Horace Greeley (1811-1872), political and social reformer, newspaper editor, and founder of the *New York Tribune* (1841); developed the *Tribune* into a widely circulated, widely read paper with a staff of distinguished writers; championed abolition, agrarian reform, and free trade

Alexander Hamilton (1755-1804), statesman and political leader; first U.S. secretary of treasury (1789); contributed to *The Federalist*, urging a strong central government and approval of the U.S. Constitution; killed in a duel with political rival Aaron Burr

William Averell Harriman (1891-1986), born in New York City; businessman, statesman, politician; governor (1955-59); advisor to Presidents Truman, Kennedy, and Johnson; ambassador to the Soviet Union (1943-46); ambassador to Great Britain (1946); ambassador at large (1961 and 1965-69); chief U.S. negotiator at the Paris peace talks to end the Vietnam War (1968-69)

Joseph Heller (1923-   ), born in Brooklyn; author whose novel *Catch-22* (1961) added a new phrase to American English; a "Catch-22" is a dilemma created by contradictory or illogical rules or conditions

Robert Henri (1865-1929), painter and art teacher; known for realistic street-life scenes; formed a loose group of artists whose subject matter gave them the name the "Ashcan School"

Edward Hopper (1882-1967), born in Nyack; artist best known for *Nighthawks* and other realistic paintings of street scenes

Lena Horne (1917-   ), born in New York City; singer; her sophisticated style helped change the stereotyped image of black performers; performed in the films *Stormy Weather* (1943) and *Words and Music* (1948); awarded the 1982 Spingarn Medal

Charles Evans Hughes (1862-1948), born in Glens Falls; jurist, statesman; governor (1906-10); U.S. Supreme Court justice (1930-41) who ruled many of President Franklin Roosevelt's New Deal laws unconstitutional

GEORGE GERSHWIN

HORACE GREELEY

ALEXANDER HAMILTON

LENA HORNE

HENRY JAMES

JOHN JAY

FIORELLO LₐGUARDIA

CLARE BOOTHE LUCE

Washington Irving (1783-1859), born in New York City; author; best known for the stories "Rip Van Winkle" and "The Legend of Sleepy Hollow," and for *Knickerbocker's History of New York*

Henry James (1843-1916), born in New York City; author; his psychological short stories and novels include *The Ambassadors* (1903) and *Washington Square*

Jacob Koppel Javits (1904-1986), born in New York City; politician; New York State congressman (1946-54); state attorney general (1954); U.S. senator (1956-80); in 1962 he polled more votes than any other politician in any state in the nation

John Jay (1745-1829), born in New York City; jurist and statesman; first chief justice of the U.S. Supreme Court (1790-95); governor (1795-1801); helped negotiate the Treaty of Paris (1783), which ended the American Revolution

Fiorello Henry LaGuardia (1882-1947), born in New York City; mayor of New York City (1934-45); his short stature, social reform programs, honest administration, and Italian surname earned him the affectionate nickname "The Little Flower"

Jack F. Kemp (1935-   ), professional football player, politician; quarterback and captain of the American Football League (AFL) Buffalo Bills; named AFL Player of the Year in 1965; U.S. representative (1971-   )

Walter Lippman (1889-1974), born in New York City; political philosopher and journalist; received a 1958 Pulitzer citation for his "Today and Tomorrow" column in the *New York Herald Tribune* (1931-67); received the 1962 Pulitzer Prize for international reporting

Robert R. Livingston (1746-1813), born in New York City; patriot and statesman; helped draft the Declaration of Independence; minister to France (1801-04); negotiated the Louisiana Purchase

Clare Boothe Luce (1903-1987), born in New York City; politician and playwright; best known for her control of the New York-based *Time-Life* publishing empire (inherited from her husband), and as one of the first U.S. women appointed to a major diplomatic post, the ambassadorship to Italy (1953-56)

Charles "Mickey" Mantle (1931-   ), professional baseball player; New York Yankees center fielder (1951-68); was the American League's Most Valuable Player four times; elected to the National Baseball Hall of Fame in 1974

George Meany (1894-1980), born in New York City; labor leader; first president of the combined American Federation of Labor and Congress of Industrial Organizations (A.F.L.-C.I.O., 1955-79); awarded the 1963 Presidential Medal of Freedom

Herman Melville (1819-1891), born Herman Melvill in New York City; novelist; best known for the classic tales *Moby Dick, or The Whale* (1851) and *Billy Budd* (first published 1924)

James Albert Michener (1907-   ), born in New York City; author; *Tales of the South Pacific* received a 1948 Pulitzer Prize and became the basis for a Broadway musical and Hollywood film, *South Pacific*; other books include *Hawaii* and *The Bridges at Toko Ri*

Arthur Miller (1915-   ), born in New York City; playwright; received the 1949 Pulitzer Prize in drama for *Death of a Salesman*

Henry Miller (1891-1980), born in New York City; author; his novel *Tropic of Cancer* (1934), banned in the U.S. until 1961, raised a controversy over the issues of censorship and pornography

Gouverneur Morris (1752-1816), born in Morrisania; patriot and statesman; helped draft the U.S. Constitution; served in the Second Continental Congress (1778-79); minister to France (1792-94); U.S. senator (1800-03)

Grandma Moses (1860-1961), born Anna Mary Robertson in Washington County; primitive painter of rural New York scenes; began painting at the age of seventy-six; had a show of her works at New York City's Museum of Modern Art

Daniel Patrick Moynihan (1927-   ), scholar and public official; grew up in New York City; U.S. ambassador to the U.N. (1975 and 1976); ambassador to India (1973-75); U.S. senator (1977-   ); wrote many influential books analyzing the problems of minority groups and of urban life

Joseph William (Joe) Namath (1943-   ), professional football player; New York Jets quarterback (1965-77) who led the team to a Super Bowl upset victory in 1969

Adolph Simon Ochs (1858-1935), newspaper publisher; took over a bankrupt *New York Times* in 1896 and turned it into one of the world's leading newspapers with a policy of thorough, nonsensational, and nonpartisan journalism

Eugene Gladstone O'Neill (1888-1953), born in New York City; playwright; received the 1936 Nobel Prize in literature; received Pulitzer Prizes in drama for *Beyond the Horizon* (1920), *Anna Christie* (1922), *Strange Interlude* (1928), and *Long Day's Journey into Night* (1957)

Joseph Pulitzer (1847-1911), journalist and newspaper publisher; bought the *New York World* (1883); founded and endowed Columbia University's Pulitzer School of Journalism; established the annual Pulitzer Prizes

Frederic Remington (1861-1909), born in Canton; artist; his paintings, drawings, and sculptures of cowboys and Indians captured the flavor of life in the American West

John D. Rockefeller (1839-1937), born in Richford, near Ithaca; industrialist and philanthropist; established the Standard Oil Company in 1870; donated some $550 million during his lifetime to such organizations as the Rockefeller Foundation and Rockefeller University

JAMES MICHENER

GRANDMA MOSES

JOSEPH PULITZER

JOHN D. ROCKEFELLER

NELSON ROCKEFELLER

ELEANOR ROOSEVELT

FRANKLIN D. ROOSEVELT

THEODORE ROOSEVELT

Nelson Aldrich Rockefeller (1908-1979), politician; governor of New York (1959-73); vice-president of the United States (1974-77)

Norman Rockwell (1894-1978), born in New York City; artist; known for his *Saturday Evening Post* magazine cover illustrations of everyday people in everyday, usually humorous, situations

Richard Rodgers (1902-1979), born in New York City; composer; he helped raise the standards of musical comedy in the U.S. with such works as *Oklahoma!* (1943), *South Pacific* (1949), *The King and I* (1951), and *The Sound of Music* (1959)

(Anna) Eleanor Roosevelt (1884-1962), born in New York City; author, diplomat, humanitarian; wife of President Franklin D. Roosevelt; acted as the president's emissary on trips in the U.S. and abroad; championed civil rights and social reform; U.S. delegate to the U.N. (1945-51)

Franklin Delano Roosevelt (1882-1945), born in Hyde Park; thirty-second president of the United States (1933-45); governor (1928-32); as president, planned New Deal legislation of federal control of industry and federal funding of public-works projects and social relief to bring the nation out of the Great Depression; after the December 7, 1941 Japanese attack on the U.S. naval and air base at Pearl Harbor during World War II, asked Congress to declare that the U.S. was at war with Japan

Theodore Roosevelt (1858-1919), born in New York City; twenty-sixth president of the United States (1901-09); commander of the Rough Riders in Cuba during the Spanish American War (1898); governor of New York (1899-1900); vice-president of the United States (1900); first American awarded a Nobel Peace Prize (1906); presidential policies included limiting the power of big business, conservation of forests and other natural resources, and beginning the building of the Panama Canal

Elihu Root (1845-1937), born in Clinton; lawyer and statesman; U.S. secretary of war (1899); U.S. secretary of state (1905-09); U.S. senator (1909-15); helped plan the League of Nations' World Court; awarded the 1912 Nobel Peace Prize

Damon Runyon (1884-1946), sportswriter for the *New York American* (after 1911); best known for comic stories of sporting and gangster street life in New York City, including the collection of tales called *Guys and Dolls* (1931)

George Herman (Babe) Ruth (1895-1948), professional baseball player; New York Yankees outfielder (1920-34); his 1927 record of 60 home runs in one season lasted until 1961; his record of 714 career home runs was not broken until 1974; member of the National Baseball Hall of Fame

Jonas Edward Salk (1914-   ), born in New York City; research scientist who developed the first effective vaccine against poliomyelitis (1953)

William Howard Schuman (1910-   ), born in New York City; educator and symphonic, ballet, and choral music composer; president of New York City's Juilliard School of Music (1945-62) and Lincoln Center for the Performing Arts (1962-69)

Peter (Pete) Seeger (1919-   ), born in New York City; folk-song composer and performer; performed with the Weavers (1940s-50s); best-known composition is "Where Have All the Flowers Gone?"

Saint Elizabeth Ann Seton (1774-1821), religious leader; founded U.S. branch of Sisters of Charity; was designated a saint of the Roman Catholic Church in 1975

Beverly Sills (1929-   ), born Belle Silverman in New York City; stage and recording opera soprano; joined the New York City Opera in 1955; retired from singing in 1980; general manager NYC Opera (1980-88); board president (1988-   )

(Marvin) Neil Simon (1927-   ), born in New York City, playwright; best known for *Barefoot in the Park* (1963) and *The Odd Couple* (1965); wrote the stories for the musicals *Sweet Charity* (1966) and *They're Playing Our Song* (1979)

Alfred Emanuel (Al) Smith (1873-1944), born in New York City; political leader; governor (1919-20, 1923-28); unsuccessful 1928 Democratic party nominee for president

Stephen Sondheim (1930-   ), born in New York City; composer and author of musical comedies; received the 1985 Pulitzer Prize in drama for *Sunday in the Park with George*

Elizabeth Cady Stanton (1815-1902), born in Johnstown; early leader of the women's rights movement; an organizer of the first women's rights convention in the U.S. (at Seneca Falls, 1848); a founder and first president (1869-90) of the National Woman Suffrage Association

Catherine Tekakwitha (1656-1680), born in Ossernenon (now Auriesville); Christian Mohawk Indian called the "Lily of the Mohawks"; entered as a candidate for sainthood in the Roman Catholic Church (1932), the first North American Indian so honored

Samuel Jones Tilden (1814-1886), born in New Lebanon; lawyer; led the attack on the corrupt Tweed Ring in New York City; governor (1875); left $3 million to found the New York City Public Library

Sojourner Truth (1797-1883), born Isabella Baumfree, in slavery, near Kingston; social reformer and powerful orator; spoke out against slavery and on behalf of women's rights

William Marcy (Boss) Tweed (1823-1878), born in New York City; political boss and founder of the Tweed Ring, which swindled New York City out of millions of dollars in city improvement funds

PETE SEEGER

ELIZABETH ANN SETON

AL SMITH

SAMUEL JONES TILDEN

MARTIN VAN BUREN

Martin Van Buren (1782-1862), born in Kinderhook; eighth president of the United States (1837-41); U.S. senator (1821-28); governor (1828); U.S. secretary of state (1828-31); vice-president of the United States (1832-36)

Cornelius (Commodore) Vanderbilt (1794-1877), born in Port Richmond on Staten Island; steamship-line and railroad industrialist

James John (Jimmy) Walker (1881-1946), born in New York City; "Roaring Twenties" mayor of New York City (1926-32)

Walt Whitman (1819-1892), born in West Hills, Long Island; author; best known for collection of poems *Leaves of Grass* and for two poems on the death of Abraham Lincoln, "O Captain! My Captain!" and "When Lilacs Last in the Dooryard Bloom'd"

GOVERNORS

George Clinton	1777-1795	Alonzo B. Cornell	1880-1882
John Jay	1795-1801	Grover Cleveland	1883-1885
George Clinton	1801-1804	David B. Hill	1885-1891
Morgan Lewis	1804-1807	Roswell P. Flower	1892-1894
Daniel D. Tompkins	1807-1817	Levi P. Morton	1895-1896
John Tayler	1817	Frank S. Black	1897-1898
De Witt Clinton	1817-1822	Theodore Roosevelt	1899-1900
Joseph C. Yates	1823-1824	Benjamin B. Odell, Jr.	1901-1904
De Witt Clinton	1825-1828	Frank W. Higgins	1905-1906
Nathaniel Pitcher	1828	Charles Evans Hughes	1907-1910
Martin Van Buren	1829	Horace White	1910
Enos T. Throop	1829-1832	John A. Dix	1911-1912
William L. Marcy	1833-1838	William Sulzer	1913
William H. Seward	1839-1842	Martin Glynn	1913-1914
William C. Bouck	1843-1844	Charles S. Whitman	1915-1918
Silas Wright	1845-1846	Alfred E. Smith	1919-1920
John Young	1847-1848	Nathan L. Miller	1921-1922
Hamilton Fish	1849-1850	Alfred E. Smith	1923-1928
Washington Hunt	1851-1852	Franklin D. Roosevelt	1929-1932
Horatio Seymour	1853-1854	Herbert H. Lehman	1933-1942
Myron H. Clark	1855-1856	Charles Poletti	1942
John A. King	1857-1858	Thomas E. Dewey	1943-1954
Edwin D. Morgan	1859-1862	W. Averell Harriman	1955-1958
Horatio Seymour	1863-1864	Nelson A. Rockefeller	1959-1973
Reuben E. Fenton	1865-1868	Malcolm Wilson	1973-1974
John T. Hoffman	1869-1872	Hugh Carey	1975-1982
John Adams Dix	1873-1874	Mario M. Cuomo	1983-
Samuel J. Tilden	1875-1876		
Lucius Robinson	1877-1879		

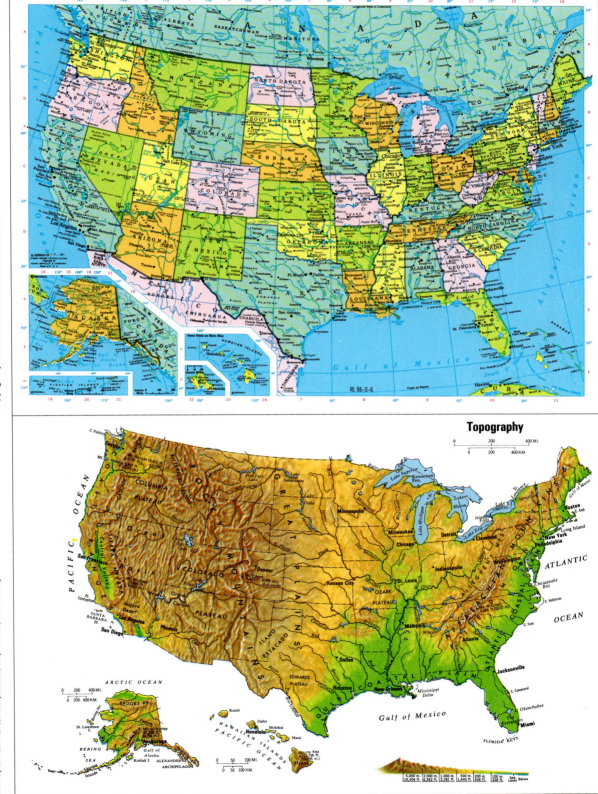

Topography

MAP KEY

Place	Coord
Adirondack Mountains	A,B6,7,f10,11
Albany	C2
Allegany Indian Reservation	C7
Allegheny Reservoir (reservoir)	C2
Alma Hill (hill)	C2
Amagansett	n16
Amsterdam	C6
Antwerp	A5,f9
Ashokan	D9
Ashokan Reservoir (reservoir)	C11
Atlantic Ocean	k12,13,n15,16,17
Auburn	C4
Ausable River (river)	B6
Beaver River (river)	A,B4,5
Binghamton	C5
Black Lake (lake)	f9
Black River (river)	A,B4,5
Block Island Sound (sound)	m16,17
Blue Mountain (mountain)	B5
Brentwood	E7,n15
Brighton	B3
Brockport	B3
Buffalo	C2
Canandaigua Lake (lake)	C3
Canisteo River (river)	C3
Cannonsville Reservoir (reservoir)	C5
Cape Vincent	A4
Carry Falls Reservoir (reservoir)	f10
Catskill Mountains (mountains)	C1,2
Cattaraugus Creek (creek)	C2
Cattaraugus Indian Reservation	C2
Cayuga Lake (lake)	C4
Cazenovia River (river)	C4
Centereach	n15
Central Islip	n15
Chautauqua	C1
Chautauqua Lake (lake)	C1
Cheektowaga	B7
Clemons	B7
Clifton Springs	B5
Clinton	C3,4
Cohocton River (river)	C7
Cohoes	f10
Colton	f10
Coney Island (island)	k13
Constantia	B4
Cooperstown	C6
Copake	C7
Corbett	C5
Corning	C3
Cranberry Lake	A6,f10
Cranberry Lake (lake)	A6
Dutchogue	m16
Dayton	C2
De Kalb	f9
De Kalb Junction	f9
Deer Park	n15
Delaware River (river)	C5,D5,6
Delaware River, East Branch (river)	D5,C5,6
Delaware River, West Branch (river)	C5,6
Delta Reservoir (reservoir)	B5
Depauville	A4
Derby	C2
Diamond Point	B7
Dover Plains	A7
Dover Mountain (mountain)	D7
Dwight D. Eisenhower Lock (lock)	f9

Place	Coord
Eagle	C2
Eagle Bridge	C7
East Hampton	n16
East Meredith	C6
East River (river)	k13
Eastport	n16
Eaton	C6
Edinburg	B6
Ellisburg	B4
Elmira	C4
Endicott	C5
Endwell	k13
Etna	C4
Fine	A5,f9
Fishers Island (island)	m16
Fonda	C6
Forestport	B5
Fort Covington	f10
Fort Miller	B7
Freeport	n15
Fulton	B4
Fultonham	C6
Gabriels	B6
Galloo Island (island)	A4
Gansevoort	C6
Gardiners Island (island)	m16,17
Genesee River (river)	C3
Geneva	B4
Genoa	C4
Georgetown	C1,2
Giant Mountain (mountain)	A7
Gilboa	C6
Glenfield	B5
Glens Falls	B7
Grafton	C7
Grahamsville	D6
Grand Gorge	C6
Grass River (river)	f10
Great Scandaga Lake (reservoir)	B7
Greenwood	C3
Greenwood Lake (lake)	D6
Greig	B5
Griffiss Air Force Base	C4,5
Groveland	C3
Haines Falls	C7
Hamburg	C2
Hamilton	C5
Hamilton Mountain (mountain)	B6
Hammond	f9
Hampton	B7
Hannawa Falls	f10
Hartford	B7
Hartwick	C6
Helena	f10
Hemlock	C3
Hempstead	n15
Henderson	B4
Henrietta	B3
Hicksville	n15
Hillsdale	C7
Himrod	C4
Hinckley Reservoir (reservoir)	B5
Hinsdale	C2
Holland	C2
Homer	C4
Hoosic River (river)	B7
Hopewell Junction	D7
Hopkinton	f9
Howard	C3

Place	Coord
Hudson	C7
Hudson River (river)	B,C,D,E7;g13,h12,13,k12;m15,n14,15
Hume	C2
Hunter Mountain (mountain)	C7
Huntersfield Mountain (mountain)	C6
Huntington	E17,n15
Hyde Park	D7
Independence River (river)	B5
Indian Lake	B6
Indian Lake (lake)	B6
Indian River (river)	A5
Inwood	k13
Irondequoit	B3
Irvington	g13
Ithaca	C4
Jamaica Bay (bay)	k13
Jamestown	C1
Jay	B6
Jefferson	C6
Johnsburg	B6
Johnson City	C5
Johnsville	B6
Keene	B6
Keene Valley	A7,f11
Kempshall Mountain (mountain)	A7,f11
Kendall	A6
Kennedy	B2
Kensico Reservoir (reservoir)	g13
Kerhonkson	D6
Keuka Lake (lake)	C3
King Ferry	A5,f9
La Fargeville	C4
Lafayette	C4
Lake Bonaparte	A5
Lake Candlewood (reservoir)	A7
Lake Champlain (lake)	B7
Lake Delta	A,B,7,f11
Lake Erie (lake)	B5,C1,2
Lake George (lake)	B7
Lake Huntington (lake)	D5,6
Lake Luzerne	B7
Lake Ontario (lake)	A,B6
Lake Placid	B6
Lake Placid (lake)	f10,11
Lancaster	f10,11
Lawrence	n15
Lawrenceville	B4
Leon	C6
Leonardsville	C1
Levittown	n15
Lewis	B4
Lewiston	B1
Lexington	C6
Lindenhurst	n15
Little Falls	B6
Little Moose Mountain (mountain)	B2
Long Beach	A7
Long Eddy	7,k13,n15
Long Island (island)	B5
Long Island Sound (sound)	E6,7,h13,k12,13,m16,17,n14,15,16; D,E7,m,n15,16
Long Lake	A7,f11
Long Lake Mountains (mountains)	B1,2,3,4,A4
Loon Lake	B6
Lower New York Bay (bay)	f10,11
Lowville	B5
Lycoming	B4
Lyon Mountain (mountain)	D6
Machias	C2
Madison	C6
Madrid	f9
Maine	C5
Manhattan (island)	h12
Marion	B3
Marlboro	D7
Martinsburg	B5
Masonville	C5
Mastic Beach	n16
McDonough	C5
Medina	B2
Meridian	B4
Middle Granville	B7
Middlesex	C3
Middletown	D6
Millbrook	D7
Milton	D7
Minerva	B6
Minetto	B4
Modena	D7
Mohawk	C5
Mohawk River (river)	B4
Monroe	D7

Place	Coord
Montauk	m17
Moose River (river)	B5
Moriah	A7
Morley	f9
Mount Kisco	D7,m15
Mount Marcy (mountain)	A7
Mount Morris (mountain)	A6
Mount Upton	C5
Mount Vernon	h13
Mountain Dale	D6
Napanoch	D5
Narrowsburg	A5
Natural Bridge	C4
Nedrow	C4
Neversink Reservoir (reservoir)	D6
Neversink River (river)	D6
New Baltimore	C7
New Bremen	B5
New City	D7,m15
New Haven	B4
New Lebanon	C7
New Rochelle	E7,h13,n15
New Woodstock	C5
New York	E7,h13,n15
New York State Barge Canal	B2,3,4,5,6
Newark	B3
Newburgh	D6
Newcomb	B6
Newton Falls	A6,f10
Niagara Falls	B1
Niagara River (river)	B1
Nicholville	f10
Nile	C2
North Bangor	f10
North Collins	C2
North Hudson	B7
North Lawrence	f10
North Norwich	C5
North Pitcher	C5
North Rose	B4
North Syracuse	B4
North Tarrytown	g13,m15
North Tonawanda	B2
Ogdensburg	f9
Old Forge	B6
Olmstedville	B7
Onchiota	f10
Oneida Lake (lake)	B4,5
Onondaga Indian Reservation	C4
Orient	m16
Orwell	B4,5
Oswegatchie	A5
Oswegatchie River (river)	f9
Oswego	B4
Oswego River (river)	B4
Otisco Lake (lake)	C5
Otsego Lake (lake)	B6
Otter Lake	B5
Owasco Lake (lake)	C4
Palenville	C6
Parishville	D6
Parksville	D6
Patterson	D7
Paul Smiths	f10
Pavilion	B6
Peekskill	A,B6
Pennellville	B4
Pepacton Reservoir (reservoir)	f10
Petersburg	B5
Phoenicia	C6
Pine Island	C2
Pine Plains	C7
Pinnacle (mountain)	D7
Piseco Lake (lake)	B6
Plattsburgh	f11
Plattsburgh Air Force Base	f11
Pleasant Valley	D7
Port Byron	B3
Port Ewen	D7
Port Kent	B7
Port Washington	h13
Portageville	C3
Porter Corners	B6
Portland	C1
Portlandville	C6
Pottersville	B6
Poughkeepsie	D7
Prattsburg	C3
Pulaski	B4
Putnam Station	B7
Pyrites	f9
Raquette Lake	B6
Raquette Lake (lake)	B6
Raquette River (river)	D6,m14

Place	Coord
Reading Center	C4
Redfield	B5
Redford	f11
Redwood	A5,f9
Rensselaerville	C6
Retsof	D7,m15
Richford	A7
Richland	A6
Richmondville	C5
Rochester	h13
Rockland	D6
Rockville Centre	B5
Rome	B5
Romulus	C4
Rossie	D6
Roxbury	C6
Rushford	C2
Russell	B5
Sacandaga Lake (lake)	B6
Sag Harbor	D7,m15
Saint Lawrence River (river)	A4,5,f8,9,10
Saint Regis Falls	C5
Saint Regis Indian Reservation	E7,h13,n15
Saint Regis River (river)	C5
Saint Regis River, West Branch (river)	E7,h13,n15
Salisbury Center	B2,3,4,5,6
Salmon River (river)	B3
Salmon River Reservoir (reservoir)	D6
Sandusky	B6
Santanoni Peak (mountain)	A6,f10
Saranac	B1
Saranac Lakes (lakes)	B1
Saranac River (river)	f10
Saratoga National Historic Park	C2
Saratoga Lake (lake)	C2
Saratoga Springs	B7
Scarsdale	f10
Schenectady	C5
Schoharie Creek (creek)	C6
Schroon Lake	C7
Schroon Lake (lake)	B7
Schuyler Lake	B4
Scio	D7,g13,m15
Seneca Falls	f9
Seneca Lake (lake)	B6
Sharon Springs	B7
Shawangunk Mountains (mountains)	f10
Shelter Island	B4,5
Sherman	C4
Shushan	m16
Sidney Center	B7
Silver Bay	B4,5
Sinclairville	A5
Skaneateles Lake (lake)	f9
Slide Mountain (mountain)	B4
Smithtown	B5
Smithville Flats	C5
Snowy Mountain (mountain)	B6
South Glens Falls	B7
Staten Island (island)	C4
Statue of Liberty National Monument	C6
Stillwater Reservoir (reservoir)	D6
Stony Island (island)	k12
Susquehanna River (river)	B5,6
Syracuse	C5,6
Tarrytown	D7,m15
Tenant Mountain (mountain)	B6
Thousand Islands (islands)	A4,5,f8,9
Tioughnioga River (river)	C4,5
Tonawanda Indian Reservation	B2
Troy	C7
Tupper Lake (lake)	A6
Tuscarora Indian Reservation	B1,2
Twin Lakes Mountain (mountain)	B6
Unadilla River (river)	C5
United Nations Headquarters	f11
Utica	B5
Valley Stream	k13,n15
Virgil	C4
Wading River	n16
Wallkill River (river)	D6
Wanakena	A6
Watertown	B4
Wayland	C3
West Canada Creek (creek)	B5
West Hampton	B6
West Point (U.S. Military Academy)	D7
West Seneca	C2
White Plains	D7,g13,m15
Whiteface Mountain (mountain)	f10
Whitney Point Lake (lake)	C5
Williamstown	B5
Woodstock	C6
Yonkers	E7,h13,n15
Yorkshire	C2

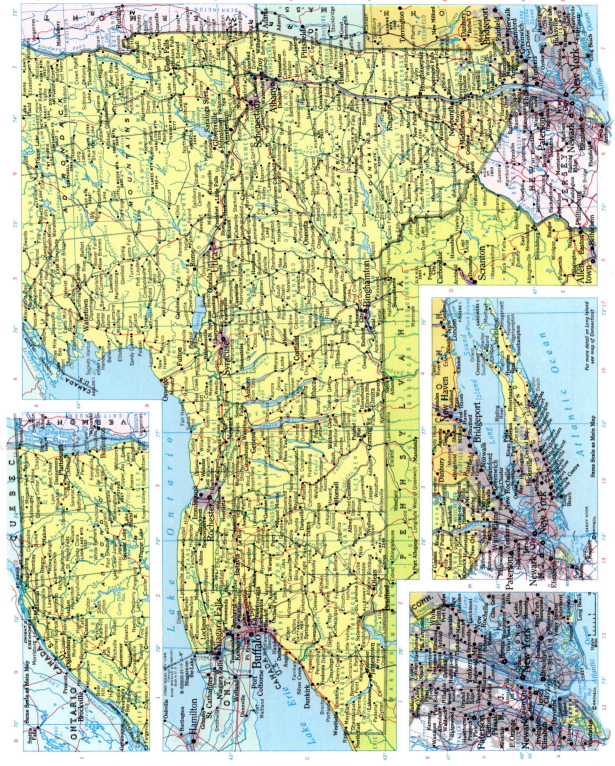

Lambert Conformal Conic Projection

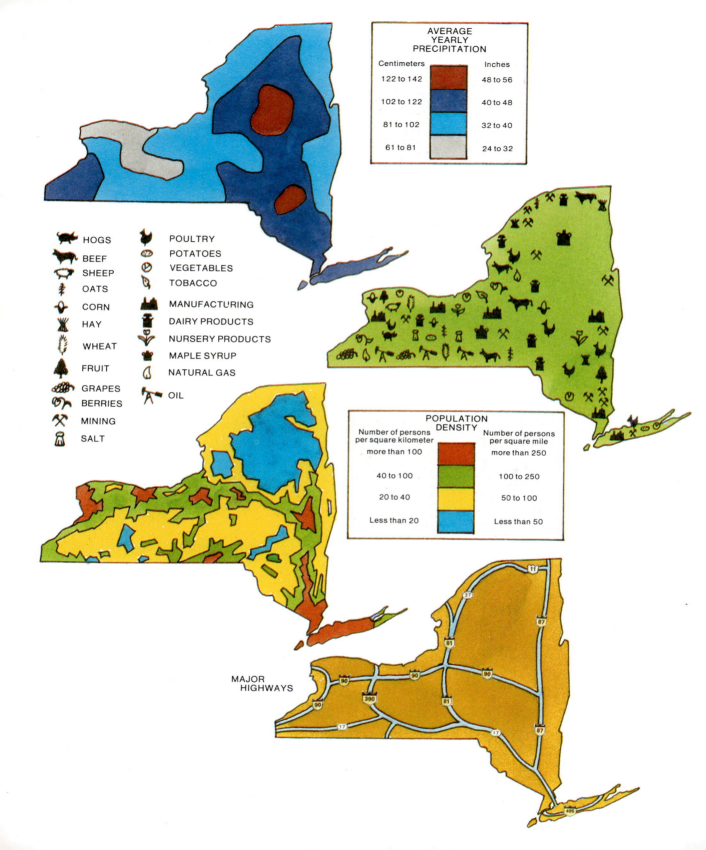

AVERAGE
YEARLY
PRECIPITATION

Centimeters		Inches
122 to 142		48 to 56
102 to 122		40 to 48
81 to 102		32 to 40
61 to 81		24 to 32

HOGS
BEEF
SHEEP
OATS
CORN
HAY
WHEAT
FRUIT
GRAPES
BERRIES
MINING
SALT

POULTRY
POTATOES
VEGETABLES
TOBACCO
MANUFACTURING
DAIRY PRODUCTS
NURSERY PRODUCTS
MAPLE SYRUP
NATURAL GAS
OIL

POPULATION
DENSITY

Number of persons per square kilometer		Number of persons per square mile
more than 100		more than 250
40 to 100		100 to 250
20 to 40		50 to 100
Less than 20		Less than 50

MAJOR
HIGHWAYS

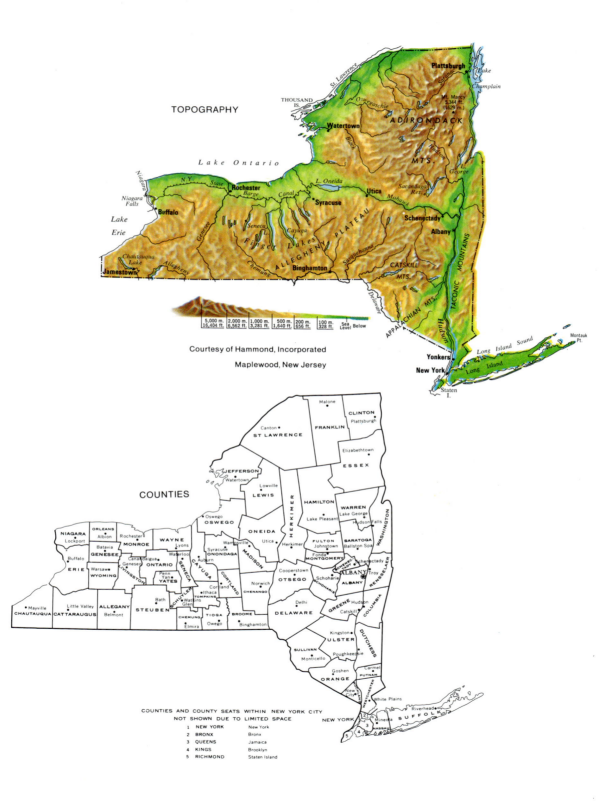

TOPOGRAPHY

Plattsburgh
Lake
Champlain
St. Lawrence
THOUSAND
IS.
Oswegatchie
Mt. Marcy
5,344 ft.
(1629 m.)
Watertown
ADIRONDACK
Black
MTS.
Hudson
L.
George
Lake Ontario
N.Y.
State
Rochester
L. Oneida
Sacandaga Res.
Niagara
Canal
Barge
Utica
Mohawk
Syracuse
Schenectady
Seneca
Cayuga
Niagara
Falls
Buffalo
Genesee
Finger
Lakes
ALLEGHENY
PLATEAU
Albany
CATSKILL
Susquehanna
Lake
Erie
Chautauqua
Lake
Allegheny
Chemung
ALLEGHENY
Binghamton
MTS.
TACONIC MOUNTAINS
Jamestown
Delaware
APPALACHIAN MTS.
Hudson
Long Island Sound
Montauk
Pt.
Yonkers
New York
Long Island
Staten
I.

5,000 m.	2,000 m.	1,000 m.	500 m.	200 m.	100 m.	Sea	Below
16,404 ft.	6,562 ft.	3,281 ft.	1,640 ft.	656 ft.	328 ft.	Level	

Courtesy of Hammond, Incorporated

Maplewood, New Jersey

COUNTIES

Malone
CLINTON
ST LAWRENCE
FRANKLIN
Plattsburgh
Canton
Elizabethtown
ESSEX
JEFFERSON
Watertown
Lowville
LEWIS
Oswego
HAMILTON
WARREN
Lake George
Oswego
OSWEGO
HERKIMER
Lake Pleasant
Hudson Falls
NIAGARA
ORLEANS
Rochester
WAYNE
ONEIDA
WASHINGTON
Lockport
Albion
Lyons
Utica
FULTON
SARATOGA
Batavia
MONROE
Wampsville
Herkimer
Johnstown
Ballston Spa
GENESEE
Syracuse
MADISON
Fonda
Buffalo
Canandaigua
ONONDAGA
MONTGOMERY
Schenectady
Waterloo
Geneseo
Auburn
ALBANY
Troy
ERIE
Warsaw
ONTARIO
Penn
Cooperstown
Schoharie
ALBANY
WYOMING
LIVINGSTON
SENECA
Yan
YATES
CAYUGA
CORTLAND
Norwich
OTSEGO
RENSSELAER
Ithaca
Cortland
CHENANGO
TOMPKINS
Watkins
Mayville
Little Valley
ALLEGANY
Bath
Glen
Delhi
GREENE
Hudson
CHAUTAUQUA
CATTARAUGUS
STEUBEN
SCHUYLER
DELAWARE
Catskill
COLUMBIA
Belmont
CHEMUNG
TIOGA
BROOME
Elmira
Owego
Binghamton
Kingston
DUTCHESS
ULSTER
Poughkeepsie
SULLIVAN
Carmel
Monticello
PUTNAM
Goshen
White Plains
ORANGE
WESTCHESTER
Riverhead
New
City
SUFFOLK
NEW YORK
Mineola
NASSAU

COUNTIES AND COUNTY SEATS WITHIN NEW YORK CITY
NOT SHOWN DUE TO LIMITED SPACE

1	NEW YORK	New York
2	BRONX	Bronx
3	QUEENS	Jamaica
4	KINGS	Brooklyn
5	RICHMOND	Staten Island

Many Manhattan apartment dwellers cultivate rooftop gardens, about the only space in the city that is available for such projects.

INDEX

Page numbers that appear in boldface type indicate illustrations.

Residents of the historic Dakota apartment building (left) have the pleasure of seeing the seasons change in Central Park.

Picture Identifications

Front cover: New York City skyline at night
Back cover: The Adirondack Mountains at Keene Valley
Pages 2-3: Heart Lake, in the Adirondacks
Page 6: The Statue of Liberty and the Manhattan skyline
Pages 8-9: A dairy farm in the valley, Millerton
Pages 16-17: Montage of New York residents
Pages 22-23: *Hudson the Dreamer, 1609*, an oil painting by J.L.G. Ferris of the landing of Henry Hudson
Pages 34-35: *The Battery, New York, 1855*, a panoramic painting by Samuel Waugh of immigrants landing at the Battery
Pages 46-47: The Statue of Liberty silhouetted against the twin towers of the World Trade Center
Pages 60-61: The Brooklyn Bridge
Page 60 (inset): The State Capitol, Albany
Pages 72-73: Montage of New York arts, entertainment, sports, and leisure activities
Page 86: ''Jacob's Ladder,'' near Keeseville, in the Adirondacks
Pages 96-97: Midtown Manhattan skyline along the Hudson River at dusk
Page 108: Montage showing the state flag, the state tree (sugar maple), the state fruit (apple), the state animal (beaver), and the state flower (rose)

About the Author

R. Conrad Stein was born and raised in Chicago. He began writing professionally shortly after graduating from the University of Illinois. He is the author of many books, articles, and short stories written for young readers. Over the years, Mr. Stein has visited New York on many occasions, and shortly before writing this book he toured the cities and lovely countryside of upstate New York and spent many exciting days in New York City. He agrees that New York is truly the Empire State. Mr. Stein now lives in Chicago with his wife and their daughter Janna.

Picture Acknowledgments

H. Armstrong Roberts: Pages 46-47; © Camerique: Front cover; © D. Muench: Pages 2-3, 15;
© H. Abernathy: Page 112
© **Jerome Wyckoff:** Back cover, page 16 (top left)
© **Cameramann International Ltd.:** Pages 4, 12 (two pictures), 64, 67, 94 (bottom right), 102
Third Coast Stock Source: © Jeff Lowe: Pages 5, 83 (top left), 138; © Sue Hagen: Pages 17
(bottom left), 19; © R. Lee: Page 65 (right); Regis Lefebure: Page 108 (top right)
© **SuperStock International:** Pages 6, 14, 17 (middle right), 20 (left), 54 (left), 56 (two
pictures), 69, 72 (bottom left, middle right), 84, 86, 88, 89 (left), 91 (three pictures), 93 (left),
95, 105, 106, 141
Journalism Services: © Dave Brown: Pages 8-9, 65 (left); © Rick Warner: Pages 72 (top left),
83 (bottom left), 101 (right); © Paul F. Gero: Pages 72 (bottom right), 119
© **Mary Ann Brockman:** Pages 16 (middle left), 21 (right), 54 (right), 66 (left), 72 (middle left),
73 (middle left), 87, 103
Marilyn Gartman Agency: © Erick Futran: Page 16 (bottom left); © Brent Winebrenner: Page
17 (bottom right); © Lee Balterman: Page 21 (left); © Mark E. Gibson: Page 73 (bottom left);
© Audrey Gibson: Page 92; © Gordon A. Reims: Page 93 (right); © Christy Volpe: Page 108 (top
right); © Wally Hampton: Page 108 (bottom left)
© **Chip and Rosa Maria Peterson:** Pages 16 (top right), 94 (top)
Odyssey Productions: © Charlene Wrobel: Pages 16 (bottom right), 99 (inset)
Nawrocki Stock Photo: © Richard Clement: Pages 17 (top left), 73 (top left), 79 (left); © Denise
DeLuise: Page 59 (left); © Steve Vidler: Page 59 (right); © James Blank: Pages 60-61, 104; © Jeff
Apoian: Page 73 (middle right)
© **Joseph A. DiChello, Jr.:** Pages 17 (middle left), 20 (bottom right), 83 (right), 90, 99 (top),
101 (left), 107
R/C Photo Agency: © J.M. Halama: Page 20 (top right)
© **J.L.G. Ferris, Archives of '76, Bay Village, Ohio:** Pages 22-23, 29
Historical Pictures Service, Inc., Chicago: Pages 26, 28, 33, 40, 42 (two pictures), 44 (left), 49
(middle right), 77 (two pictures), 125 (Arthur and Cleveland), 126 (Dewey), 127 (Gershwin,
Greeley, and Hamilton), 128 (Jay), 130 (E. Roosevelt, F. Roosevelt, and T. Roosevelt), 131
(Seton and Tilden)
© **Yale University Art Gallery:** Page 32
Museum of the City of New York: Pages 34-35
The Bettmann Archive, Inc.: Pages 39, 43, 44 (right), 49 (top right, top left, bottom left,
bottom right), 50 (right), 53 (two pictures), 72 (top right, middle bottom), 73 (bottom right),
81 (right), 125 (Clinton), 126 (Clinton and Eastman), 128 (James), 129 (Pulitzer and
Rockefeller), 132
U.S. Bureau of Engraving and Printing: Page 50 (left)
Root Resources: © James Blank: Pages 51, 60 (inset), 96-97, 111; © Kitty Kohout: Page 108
(tree)
UPI/Bettmann Newsphotos: Pages 58 (two pictures), 81 (left), 124, 125 (Chisholm), 126
(DiMaggio), 127 (Horne), 128 (LaGuardia and Luce), 129 (Michener and Moses), 130
(Rockefeller), 131 (Seeger and Smith)
Tom Stack & Associates: © Steve Elmore: Pages 66 (right), 79 (right), 80
Addison Gallery of American Art, Philips Academy, Andover, Massachusetts: Page 75
Giraudon/Art Resource: Page 76
Joan Dunlop: Page 89 (right)
© **Arch McLean:** Page 94 (bottom left)
Len W. Meents: Maps on pages 86, 88, 90, 92, 94, 99, 136
Courtesy Flag Research Center, Winchester, Massachusetts 01890: Flag on page 108